LANCELOT
OR THE KNIGHT OF THE CART

CHRÉTIEN DE TROYES

A Translation into English by

A. S. KLINE

Illustrated Edition

POETRY IN TRANSLATION

www.poetryintranslation.com

Please direct sales or editorial enquiries to:
tonykline@poetryintranslation.com

This print edition is published by
Poetry In Translation (*www.poetryintranslation.com*),
via Amazon Services UK Limited (a UK limited company with registration number
03223028 and its registered office at 1 Principal Place, Worship Street, London,
EC2A 2FA)

ISBN-13: 978-1794662643

CONTENTS

ABOUT THIS WORK

Chrétien de Troyes' Arthurian Romances, written in the late 12th-century, provide a vital link between the Classical Roman poets, Ovid in particular, and the later medieval world of Dante and Chaucer. The five major verse tales, namely Érec and Énide (c1170), Cligès (c1176), Yvain or the Knight of the Lion (before 1181) Lancelot or the Knight of the Cart (before 1181), and Perceval (before 1190), introduce motifs and plot elements that recur frequently in later literature. Well-structured, lively, and witty the tales were written for a sophisticated courtly audience, and the five stories considered together gave expression to the reality and the deeper ideals of French chivalry. Chrétien appears to have used themes culled from French and British sources, while characters such as Lancelot, and features such as the Holy Grail appear for the first time in European literature in his work. Here translated in rhyming couplets to mirror the original, rather than in unrepresentative prose, is a fresh treatment of one of France's and Europe's major poets.

'*This lady doth exceed the rest,*
Of all those who meet our eyes'
The Romance of King Arthur and
his Knights of the Round Table (p530, 1917)
Sir Thomas Malory (15th cent), Arthur Rackham (1867-1939)
and Alfred William Pollard (1859-1944)
Internet Archive Book Images

LINES 1-30 CHRÉTIEN'S INTRODUCTION

SINCE my Lady of Champagne,
Would have me take my quill again,
And pen a romance, I write anew,
Willingly, as a man who'd do,
Without seeking to flatter her,
All he can in the world for her.
But if one did, in such a matter,
Wish to offer praise, and flatter,
He might say, and I'd so attest,
This lady doth exceed the rest,
Of all those who meet our eyes,
Much as the breeze that doth arise
In April and May proves best of all.
I'faith, I'll not such speech recall;
Not being one to flatter his lady,
Shall I say: 'What a gem may be
Worth, in pearls and chalcedony,
The Countess is worth in royalty?'
Nay, I shall say naught I may rue,
Though, in spite of me, it is true:
But this I'll say, that her command
Has more to do with this at hand,
Than any effort that I'll bestow.
Here Chrétien begins it, though,
His book of the Knight of the Cart;
Whose matter and sense, for her part,
The Countess grants, and he but tries
To set forth, in his thoughts' guise,
Her concerns and her intention.

LINES 31-172 SIR KAY ACCEDES TO THE QUEEN'S REQUEST

I say that once, upon Ascension,
King Arthur held a worthy court,
Rich and fine as ever was sought,
For such was fitting for the day.
After dinner he chose to stay,
Not forsaking his companions;
In the room was many a baron,
And the queen was present too,
And she had with her not a few
Of her fair and courteous ladies,
Speaking French most fluently.
Kay who'd furnished the tables,
Was eating with the constables;
And there, where Kay sat to eat,
Came a knight, armed complete,
All equipped as one who fought,
And so appeared before the court.
The knight, suddenly advancing,
Came and stood before the king,
Where Arthur sat among his lords;
All form of greeting he ignored,
Saying: 'Arthur, in my prisons
I have knights, ladies, maidens,
Of your realm and your household;
But this thing to you I have told
Not that to you I may them render;
Rather I wish this truth to tender,
That you have not the power here
To regain those that you hold dear;
Know indeed that death shall find you

Before you can effect their rescue.'
The king replied that he must suffer
What he had not the power to cure,
But nonetheless it grieved him deeply.
Then the knight turned, much as if he
Wished to depart, tarrying no longer,
Not waiting for the king, but rather
Seeking out the door of the hall;
And yet, before he left them all,
Halting upon the stair, said he:
'King, if at your court there be
A knight in whom you have such trust
That the queen you'd dare entrust
To him, to lead her, after me,
Into the woods where I journey,
I promise to await him there,
And give the prisoners into his care,
Whom I hold exiled in my land,
Should he defeat me, you understand,
And bring her safely back to you.'
Many in the palace heard him too,
And the court was in commotion.
Kay listened to him, with emotion,
Where he sat with the constables.
He leaped to his feet, left the table
And went straight before the king,
As if he was in anger speaking:
'King, I have served you long indeed
Faithfully, and yet now I plead
To take my leave, and issue forth,
For I shall never serve you more.
I've no wish to attend upon
Or serve you from this moment on.'
The king was grieved by what he heard,
And, once he could summon a word,

His astonishment he expressed:
'Kay, speak you in earnest, or in jest?'
And Kay replied: 'Fair sire, indeed
For jesting I've nor taste nor need,
I request your leave most earnestly;
No other wages do I seek
Nor reward for all my service;
I have decided, my wish it is
That I depart without delay.'
'Is it through anger or spite, pray,'
Said the king: 'that you wish to go?
Seneschal, stay at court, and know,
As tis your wont to be here, so I
Possess naught in this world that I
Would not grant you most willingly
Should you consent to stay with me.'
'Sire,' said Kay, 'that will not serve;
I'd not accept, to stay and serve,
An ounce of the purest gold a day.'
Thereon, the king, in great dismay,
Hurried away, the queen to see.
'Lady, you'll not believe,' said he,
What the Seneschal doth request;
He would leave the court, I attest,
Though for what reason I know not.
Yet he will do for you, God wot,
That which he will not do for me;
So go to him now, my dear lady!
Though to stay for me he'll not deign,
Beg him for your sake to remain.
Fall at his feet, if such needs be,
For if I should lose his company
I'd never again know happiness.'
The king sends the queen, no less,
To the Seneschal; she doth light

On him among the other knights;
And, when before him, she doth say:
'I encounter great sorrow, Kay,
Surely, if this sad news be true,
That which I hear, but now, of you.
It grieves me, this, that I am hearing,
That you would wish to leave the king;
How so? And for what purpose?
I cannot think you as courteous,
Or as wise, as has been your wont;
That you should stay is what I want,
So Kay, remain, I beg of you.'
'Lady,' says he, 'my thanks to you,
But nonetheless I cannot stay.'
The queen again makes her assay,
And with her all the knights, en masse,
While Kay says he wearies, alas,
Of such unprofitable service.
The queen, at this reply of his,
Falls prostrate, at my Lord Kay's feet,
Kay now begs her to rise, but she
Says she will ne'er do so, unless
He chooses to grant her request,
And do her bidding willingly.
Kay then promises, faithfully,
If the king grants him a boon then he,
Will stay, and she must grant the same.
'Kay,' she said, 'if you will remain
We'll grant the boon, whate'er it is;
Come now, and tell him that on this,
Your sole condition, you will stay.'
So, away with the queen went Kay
And they both came before the king.
'I've prevented Kay from leaving,
Though not easily, Sire,' said she,

'On the understanding that what he
Requests of you, you will so grant.'
The king sighed with pleasure, and
Said that whate'er he might demand,
He would obey Sir Kay's command.

LINES 173-246 KING ARTHUR GRANTS KAY'S DEMAND

'SIRE,' said Kay, 'hear now what I
Desire, and the favour, in reply,
That you yourself have promised me;
Fortunate am I that you agree
To grant this boon, of your mercy.
Sire, my lady whom here you see,
You must entrust to me outright,
That we may follow the knight
Who in the forest now awaits us.'
The king is grieved, and yet he does,
For he's a man of his word, alway.
Though he cannot but display
In his face, his deep displeasure.
The queen too grieves, in full measure,
And all say what Kay has sought,
Out of pride and madness wrought,
Is an outrageous boon to grant.
But the king now, by the hand,
Takes the queen and says to her:
'My lady, now, without demur,
You must Sir Kay accompany.'
And Kay says: 'Trust her to me,
And have no fear, Sire, of aught,
For I will return her, as I ought,
To you, safe and sound, and happy.'

So the king does, so they both leave,
And all there would seek to follow,
For not one there is free of sorrow.
You should know, the Seneschal
Fully armed, for his mount did call,
Which into the courtyard, was led
Together with a palfrey, one bred
For the queen's use, exclusively.
The queen approached the palfrey,
One neither restive nor obstinate;
Then grieving, sighing at her fate,
She mounted, and close to tears,
Said to herself, so none could hear:
'Alas, if you but reflected now,
I am sure you would ne'er allow
One pace, unchallenged, I be led!'
She thought none knew what she'd said,
But Count Guinable had heard her,
Who as she mounted stood beside her.
Among them all such tears started,
Men and women, as they departed,
Twas as if she lay dead on her bier,
For they did not hope to see her
Ever again, while they still lived.
The Seneschal, tis to be believed,
Led her to where the knight waited.
But to none came the belated
Thought to follow them instead,
Until my Lord Gawain now said,
To the king, his uncle, speaking:
'Sire, you have done a foolish thing,
A thing at which I marvel greatly,
But, if you'll take counsel of me,
While they are both, as yet, nearby
We shall ride after them, you and I,

And any others who may so wish.
Since I, regarding my part in this,
Will pursue them, straight away,
As it would not be right, I say,
Not to follow, at least until
We can from it all the truth distil,
As to what has become of the queen,
Or news of Kay's intentions glean.'
'Ah, fair nephew,' the king replied,
'Your courtesy ne'er will be denied.
And since you manage this affair
Order our mounts to be prepared,
Bridled and saddled so that we
Have naught to do, but ride speedily.'

LINES 247-398 THE KNIGHT OF THE CART

THEIR horses were quickly brought,
Apparelled and saddled, to the court.
First, the king mounted amain;
And after him my Lord Gawain,
Then all the others rapidly.
Each man of that company
Then departed as he pleased.
Some of them their weapons seized,
My Lord Gawain was one of these,
While others went weapon-free;
Gawain made his two squires lead
Two extra mounts, in case of need;
As they thus approached the forest
They saw Kay's horse make egress;
All there recognised his charger,
And the reins, they saw further,

From the bridle, had been torn.
The horse seemed quite forlorn,
The stirrup straps were blood-stained,
And, though the saddle-bow remained,
The saddle was all broken behind
All there were now troubled in mind,
Nudged each other and shook their heads.
My Lord Gawain had ridden ahead,
Far in front, half a league or more,
And thus it was not long before
He saw a knight approaching slowly
On a horse panting and weary,
Sore, and covered with sweat.
The knight was first, as they met,
To offer a greeting to Gawain,
Which he then returned again.
Then the knight recognising
My Lord Gawain, and halting,
Said: 'Sire, you no doubt see
My mount is tired and weary,
Such that he is no use to me?
And those two horses that I see,
Are surely yours, so I ask of you,
Pledging that I shall return you
Both the service and the favour,
The gift or loan of whichever
You might choose to grant to me.'
Then choose whichever that you see,'
Replied Gawain, 'best pleases you.'
Of which was the finer of the two
The knight, though, took little heed,
Nor the taller, being in great need,
But swiftly leapt onto the nearer,
Rather than seeking for the fairer,
And rode away, through the forest.

'*The knight then, without taking rest,*
Now spurred away through the forest'
St. Nicholas [serial] (p695, 1873)
Mary Mapes Dodge (1830-1905)
Internet Archive Book Images

The mount he'd left, deprived of rest,
And ridden till foundered, fell dead,
Misused and wearied, as I have said.
The knight then, without taking rest,
Now spurred away through the forest,
With my Lord Gawain racing after,
Chasing and following with fervour,
Until he reached the foot of a hill.
On riding a distance further still,
He found the mount, dead outright,
Which he had gifted to the knight.
Horses had trampled the ground
And there was a scatter he found
Of shields and lances lying there.
It seemed there'd been a fierce affair
Involving several armed knights.
He, seeing he had missed the fight,
Was grieved not to have been there.
However he did not linger where
The fight had been, but went on,
Until by chance he came upon
The knight, on foot, and in haste,
All armed and with his helmet laced,
Shield at his neck, and sword girt,
Overtaking a cart, with a spurt.
(A pillory is now reserved
For the purpose a cart then served.
And where a thousand now are found
In every fine substantial town,
In those days there was only one,
And this cart was used in common
As the pillory is in our day
For those who murder and betray,
And those who commit perjury,
And those who steal property,

Thieves who snatch things from others,
Or are blatant highway robbers.
Those convicted of some crime,
Were set in the cart for a time,
And dragged through every street;
Their loss of rights was complete,
Nor in any court were they heard,
Nor welcome nor honoured there.
Since the cart was, at that day,
Regarded with such great dismay,
There was a saying: 'If you see
A cart, if such encounters thee,
Cross yourself, and loudly call
On God, lest evil doth befall.')
The knight then, without a lance,
Upon the cart doth now advance
And sees a dwarf seated aloft,
Who holds, as any carter doth,
A long goad in his two hands.
And of the dwarf the knight demands
'Dwarf, by God, now tell to me,
If you have seen the king's lady,
Go riding past you, recently.'
The wretched dwarf of low degree
Gave him not a word of news,
But said: 'If you would climb up too
Onto this cart I'm riding here,
Tomorrow you will surely hear
What has become of the queen.'
Then continued the way he'd been
Going, and gave him no more heed.
The knight took but two steps indeed,
Before he swiftly climbed aboard;
Yet ill for him, who so abhorred
The shame, that he did not so do

At once, for that he'd later rue!
Yet Reason, that's divorced from Love,
Warned him from making such a move,
Counselling him thus to refrain,
Telling him all things to disdain
That presage reproach and shame.
Reason then must share the blame,
Reaching the lips, but not the heart.
So Reason counselled, for its part;
Yet Love, enclosed within the heart,
Urged him to mount aboard the cart.
That he did, since Love wished it so,
Careless of what shame might follow,
Since it was Love's wish and command.
My Lord Gawain, now close at hand,
Spurred on and overtook the pair,
While at the knight now seated there
Wondering greatly, and said loudly
To the dwarf: 'Can thou tell me,
Aught of the queen, if you know?'
He said: 'If you hate yourself so,
Like this knight who sits by me,
Then climb aboard, if you please,
And I will carry you both along.'
When Lord Gawain heard his song,
He thought the thing a great folly,
And said he did not, nor would he,
It being shameful, for a start
To exchange a horse for a cart.
'But you go onwards, as you will,
And I will follow after still.'

LINES 399-462 THE TOWER AND THE MAID

SO onward they went journeying,
Two on the cart, and one riding,
Trundling along, all together,
Till they reached a castle at vespers;
And a fine castle, you must know,
With beauty and riches, all aglow.
And all three entered by the gate.
Its people wondered at the fate
Of the knight upon the cart,
Showing contempt, on their part,
Taunting him, both high and low,
The little children, the very old,
Shouting aloud along the street;
Thus the strange knight they greet,
With base villainy and scorn.
'To what punishment is borne
This knight?' they all enquire:
'Is he to be scorched with fire,
Hanged, drowned, or grace a heap
Of thorns? Tell us, oh dwarf, who keep
The cart, in what crime was he caught?
Is he accused of stealing aught?
Is he a thief or a murderer?'
Not a word did the dwarf utter,
Neither looking to left or right.
To lodgings he led the knight,
Closely followed by Gawain,
Off to a tower, standing plain
Above the town which lay below,
While beyond stretched a meadow;

The tower high on a rock, sheer,
Close by the town, did thus appear.
Into the tower Gawain now went,
And there in the hall an elegant
And charming maiden he did see,
The fairest maid in that country;
And two girls accompanying her,
Both noble and beautiful they were.
As soon as they saw my Lord Gawain
They greeted him, and they made plain
Their joy on welcoming him there;
Then asked, of the other knight aware:
'Dwarf, for what is this knight to blame,
That he is borne like one who's lame?'
The dwarf showed no desire to answer,
But made the knight descend the faster,
And then he and the cart withdrew;
Where he was going to none knew.
Then dismounted my Lord Gawain,
And valets then disarmed the same,
Relieving both knights of their armour.
Two green mantles the maiden ordered
To be brought, which they assumed.
When the hour for supper loomed,
A fine meal was swiftly served,
And a place was there reserved
For the maiden, beside Gawain,
Nor were the two knights fain
To change their lodging for another,
For she showed them great honour
And fine and pleasant company,
All that evening long, was she.

'*The fairest maid in that country*'
The Blue Poetry Book (p173, 1891)
Andrew Lang (1844-1912), H. J. Ford (1860-1941)
and Lancelot Speed (1860-1931)
Internet Archive Book Images

LINES 463-538 THE BED AND THE LANCE

WHEN they'd supped long enough there,
Two beds, long and high, were prepared,
In the midst of the tower hall;
And another, the fairest of all,
Was also prepared by their side;
And it, as the tales testify,
Possessed every fine quality
That in a bed could ever be.
And when the time came for rest,
The maiden led away her guests,
With a show of hospitality,
To those beds, long and wide, and she
Said to them: 'Both those beds there
To ease your bodies were prepared,
But in that further bed, say I,
Only the worthiest may lie.
It was not set there for your use.'
The knight who'd suffered the abuse
Of the cart, at once, gave answer,
Disdaining this warning from her,
And speaking to the maiden said:
'Tell me the reason why that bed
Should be forbidden, as you say.'
The maid answered, straight away,
Though she knew the reason well:
'Such things to you I may not tell
Who have no right to so enquire!
For every knight is shamed entire,
Who has been carried in that cart;
Nor is it meet that I should part

With an answer to such requests,
Nor he indeed be that bed's guest,
A thing for which he'd surely pay.
It was not made for you this day,
So richly, and so carefully.
You would indeed pay, and dearly
For ever harbouring such a thought.'
'You will soon see,' was his retort,
'I shall see?' 'Yes, now, and truly;
I know not who will pay,' said he,
'But upon my life, whoever may be
Troubled by it, or it may grieve,
I would lie down there on that bed,
And at my leisure so rest my head.'
Then he disrobed, and there did lie,
On the bed which was long and high,
Two feet higher than the other two,
Clothed with silk of yellow hue,
And a coverlet starred with gold.
The furs were neither vair nor old,
But were fresh and were of sable;
Fit for a king in some rare fable
Were the covers that graced him,
Nor was the mattress under him
Woven of rushes, nor of straw.
Yet, of a sudden, midnight saw
A lance descend from high above
As if its steel tip, falling, would
Pierce the knight through the side,
Coverlet, and white sheets beside,
And pin him there, where he lay.
And the lance a pennant displayed
Which was fair wreathed in flame,
And setting light to all that same,
Fired the coverlet and the sheets,

And the bed itself, all complete.
And the lance-tip passed so close
That it pierced the skin almost,
But without forming a deep wound.
Then the knight woke, as yet still sound,
Quenched the fire, and seized the lance,
And into the room did it advance,
Hurled it away, but kept his bed,
And once more laid down his head,
And slept as soundly, now secure,
As he'd lain down to rest before.

LINES 539-982 THE ENCOUNTER AT THE FORD

THE next morning, at break of day,
The maid of the tower, straight away,
Had the Mass said for her guests,
And bade them both rise and dress.
When for them Mass had been said,
The knight who'd in the cart been led,
Sat pensively beside a window
That looked out over the meadow,
And gazed upon the fields below.
The maid came to another window,
And there she held conversation
With my Lord Gawain stationed
There, awhile, though upon what
Subject they spoke I know not,
For I know naught of their intent;
But, while upon the sill they leant,
Through the fields, along the river,
They saw men carrying a bier,
And on the bier there lay a knight

And three maids kept it in sight,
Making a deep show of mourning.
They saw, too, a host approaching,
Behind the bier, and before it came
A tall knight. By her horses' rein,
On his left, he led a fair lady.
The knight at the window did see
And recognise she was the queen;
And, as long as she could be seen,
With close attentiveness, the knight,
Continued to gaze, in deep delight.
And when he could see her no more,
He was determined as never before
To throw himself from that height,
And he would have done so quite
Had not Lord Gawain realised
His purpose, and dragged him aside,
Saying: 'I beg you, sir, desist!
For God's sake think no more of this,
Commit you not so mad a deed!
Tis wrong to despise life, indeed.'
But: 'He is right!' the maiden cried,
'For news will travel far and wide
Of his disgrace, and it be known
How in the cart his shame was shown,
Rather he'd wish then to be dead,
Better die thus than live instead.
Life henceforth must him distress,
Filled with shame and unhappiness.'
But the knights asked for their armour,
Arming themselves, then and there,
And the maid showed them courtesy,
Regard and generosity,
For though she had mocked the knight,
And scorned him, as well she might,

She yet gave him a horse and lance,
From goodwill and kindness perchance.
Thus, politely and courteously,
The two knights took their leave,
Of the lady, saluting her,
Then, taking the path away from her,
Followed the way the host went,
Issuing forth from the castle, bent
On pursuit, and speaking to none.
Swiftly, the way the queen had gone,
They took their path, but could not make
Sufficient speed to overtake
The host that, passing quickly on,
From fields into a glade were gone;
But there they found a beaten road,
And onward through the wood they rode,
Until it might be nearly prime,
And at a crossroads, at that time,
They met a maiden there whom they
Saluted, and did ask and pray
To tell them, if indeed she knew
And might thus inform them too,
Which way the queen had been led.
She looked knowingly, and said:
'If you both pledge your word to me,
I could set you, and right swiftly,
On the true road, and so declare,
To you both, what land lies there,
And what knight it is that leads her;
But who would that same land enter
He must endure great suffering,
Before he can achieve the thing!'
Then my Lord Gawain replied:
'So help me God, fair maid, so I
Promise to you, regarding this,

That I will offer, in your service,
All my strength, as you please,
If you will tell the truth to me.'
After which, the knight of the cart,
Not merely promising, on his part,
All his strength, also proclaimed,
As might a man by Love sustained,
Empowered, and ready for aught,
That he would promise her aught
She wished, at once, without delay,
And in her service was that day.
'Then I will tell you all,' said she,
And the maid told them this story:
'I'faith, my lords, one Meleagant,
A knight as hard as adamant,
Son of the King of Gorre, has her,
And to that realm he has led her
From which no stranger doth return,
But in that country must sojourn
In exile and in servitude.'
So her tale they then pursued,
Asking: Maid, where is this land?
Where then, may we understand,
Lies this place?' And she replied:
'You shall know; yet first, say I,
Many a danger you must pass,
For to find entrance there at last
Is hard, except its king allow;
Bademagu's his name I trow.
One can enter, nevertheless,
By two paths, both perilous,
By two ways, and both appal;
One, the Sunken Bridge they call,
Because below the water it lies;
Above it doth the water rise

To the same measure as below,
As deep here as there doth flow,
Such that the bridge lies between,
But a foot and a half wide, I ween,
And the same thickness it shows.
Better to choose it not, although
It is the less perilous of the two,
Yet it brings further dangers too,
Of which I shall say naught here.
The other bridge is more to fear,
Where such great peril must be met,
That none has ever crossed it yet;
For it is like a sharpened blade,
And so its name is as tis made;
The Bridge of the Sword tis called:
And now I have told you all
The truth I can say, and know.'
But then they asked of her also:
'Fair maiden, would you now deign
To show us both the bridges plain?'
To which the maiden now replied:
'The direct way lies on this side
To the Sunken Bridge, while there
To the Bridge of the Sword you'd fare.'
Then the knight, he who had been
Borne on the cart, intervened:
'Sir,' he said, 'without prejudice,
I will grant you the choice in this,
Take whichever path you prefer
And leave the other to my care.'
'By my faith,' said my Lord Gawain,
'Both now threaten peril and pain,
Both the one and the other passage;
Which the most ill doth presage,
I know not, nor which is best,

But tis not right that I protest
When you have given me to choose.
The Sunken Bridge I'll not refuse.'
'Without more ado then, it is right,
The Bridge of the Sword,' said the knight,
'I should take, and shall, willingly.'
Thereupon they parted, all three,
Commending each other courteously
To God, while the maid said, said she,
Watching them leave: 'Remember me,
For each owes me a favour, and so be
Sure not to forget, when I do send.'
'Truly, we shall not, my sweet friend,'
Called out both the knights as one;
Then each took his path and was gone.
And he of the cart is lost in thought,
Like a man who cannot in aught
Defend himself gainst Love that binds;
And his thoughts are of such a kind
He forgets himself, like one instead
Who knows not if he's alive or dead,
Who cannot remember his own name,
Nor whether he is armed, the same,
Nor where he comes from nor goes.
For nothing do his thoughts enclose
Except one person, and she he finds
Has driven all others from his mind.
And he thinks of her so incessantly
Naught else doth he now hear or see.
And his mount bears him, at speed,
Not by some wandering path indeed
But by the best and straightest way,
Carrying him onwards all the day
Till a wide, open land, they gain.
Now, there was a ford in that plain,

And on the far side loomed in sight,
Guarding the ford, an armed knight,
And a maid was in his company,
Who'd ridden there on her palfrey.
Mid-afternoon the day did see,
But the knight of the cart still he
Tirelessly pursued his thought,
While his thirsty mount of naught
But the fine clear stream did think;
And reaching it hastened to drink.
Then he who kept the other side:
'This ford I guard, knight!' he cried,
'In case you may desire to cross.'
But in his thoughts the other lost
Neither heard him nor gave heed;
While in the meantime his steed
Had moved swiftly to the water.
The knight called to him further,
That he'd be wise to keep away,
For he'd not pass there that day;
And swore by the heart in his side
That he'd attack him if he tried.
But the other heard not his shout,
So for a third time he called out:
'Knight, do not, against my will,
Enter the ford, I'll deny you still.
Upon my life, ill shall you fare
If I should see you enter there.'
But the other still heard him not;
While, eagerly, his horse had got
Into the water, at a single leap,
Quenching its thirst, and drinking deep.
The knight declared that he must pay;
Nor would he gain in any way
From the shield and hauberk on his back;

His horse he spurred to the attack,
Urging a gallop from the steed,
And struck his enemy hard indeed,
So that our knight was upended
Amidst the ford, so well defended;
From his hand the lance now flew,
And the shield from his neck too.
Shocked, as he the water did greet,
Though stunned, he leapt to his feet,
Like a man aroused from slumber,
Listening, gazing about in wonder,
To see who might have dealt the blow.
Then facing the other knight, his foe,
He cried: 'Vassal, now tell me why
You have attacked me, speak no lie,
For you were unbeknown to me,
And I have done you no injury.'
'I'faith,' he answered, 'you wronged me,
Did you not treat me disdainfully
When I thrice forbade you the ford,
For my calls to you were ignored
Though I spoke loud as I might?
You heard me challenge you, sir knight,
Two of those three times, or more,
Yet in spite of that, entered the ford,
Though I told you that ill you'd fare
If I saw you in the water there.'
The knight of the cart then replied:
'Damned if I heard you, if you cried;
Whoever else might, I heard naught!
It may well be I was deep in thought
When you denied the ford to me;
I'll do you ill and presently
If one of my hands I can lay
On your horse's bridle today.'

And the other answered: 'What of that?
You may grasp my bridle pat
If you dare, and I so allow.
A handful of ashes I do vow
Is the worth of your threats to me.'
And he replied: 'Then we agree,
For I would lay my hands on you,
Whatever outcome might ensue.'
Then, as the knight, leaving shore,
Rode to the middle of the ford,
He seized, in his left, the bridle tight
And grasped the knight's leg with his right,
And pulled and dragged and squeezed
So roughly that the knight, displeased,
Thought that such force would surely
Tear his leg straight from his body;
And begged that he might be let go,
Calling out: 'Should it please you so,
With me, on equal terms to fight,
Then take your horse, and shield, sir knight,
And grasp your lance, and joust with me.'
The knight of the cart replied, briefly:
'T'faith, I'll not, for I think you'll flee,
As soon as ever I set you free.'
The knight, on hearing, felt great shame,
And said: 'Sir knight, now mount again,
With confidence, upon your horse,
For you shall have my oath, of course,
That I will neither flinch nor flee,
For the shame of it would trouble me.'
The knight of the cart replied once more:
'You must swear me that oath before,
And give your word most faithfully
That you will neither flinch nor flee,
Nor shall you launch any attack

Till you see me on my steed's back,
Nor shall you hover too near to me,
For I'll be treating you generously
If in my hands I yet let thee go.'
The knight could do naught but so,
And when he had heard him swear,
He seized his shield and lance there
Which were floating in the stream,
And, by this time, it would seem
Had drifted some distance away;
Then turned to mount, without delay.
Once astride, he seized his shield
And by the straps he did it wield,
And couched his lance in its rest.
Then each knight the other did test,
Spurring his mount to full speed,
Though he who kept the ford indeed
Was the first to strike his enemy
And attacked his man so fiercely
That his lance was splintered quite;
Yet engaged by the latter knight,
And thrown prostrate in the ford
Twas over him the water poured.
Then the knight of the cart withdrew
Dismounting, thinking he could hew
And drive a hundred such away.
If his sword he brought in play,
The other leapt up and also drew
His gleaming blade, fine and new.
There they clashed, hand to hand,
Shield before, each made his stand,
On which the gold glittered bright,
Wielding their swords with might,
Never resting, warring ceaselessly.
They landed many a blow, bravely,

And for so long the fight sustained,
The knight of the cart felt ashamed,
In his heart's depth, at how badly
He'd fared on a path chosen freely,
If having elected to go this way
He'd yet encountered such delay
In conquering a single knight.
For if a hundred such he might
Have met with the previous day
They must surely have given way;
Yet now he was angered and grieved,
To be so weary, since he perceived
His blows fell short, the day waned;
Thus he ran at the other, and so gained
Upon him that the other knight fled;
Leaving, reluctantly, in his stead,
The ford unguarded, its passage free.
But the knight of the cart eagerly
Chased the man till he fell to his knees,
And then he swore by all he could see
That the man should rue that day
When he'd upset him on his way
And had so disturbed his reverie.
She, of the knight's company,
The maid who'd ridden at his side,
Heard this threat and more beside;
Filled with fear, she begged that he
For her sake, would grant him mercy.
But he replied he could not do so,
No drop of mercy could he show,
Since he had suffered such shame.
Then, with drawn sword, once again
He neared the knight, who, in dismay,
Cried: 'For mine and for God's sake,
Grant me the mercy I ask of you.'

And he replied: 'God's love, tis true
No man shall e'er sin against me
To whom I would not show mercy,
For God's sake, if on God he call,
One time at least, if it so befall.
Now therefore I must grant it, too
Since I ought not to deny it you,
When you've asked it thus of me;
But give me your word faithfully
To be my prisoner whenever I
Shall summon you to me, thereby.'
This he did, though reluctantly.
The maiden then said, right swiftly:
'Since, of your goodness, sir knight,
You have granted, as if of right,
Mercy to him, as he begged you,
Then if you free all prisoners too,
Release this prisoner to me.
At my request now, set him free,
On condition that, come the day,
I'll do all I can to repay
You in any way you please.'
The knight of the cart then agreed,
Accepting all she promised there,
And freed the knight into her care;
Though she was yet in some bother,
Lest he might now recognise her,
Which was a thing she wished not;
But he departed, and lingered not.
So to God they commended him,
And thus they took their leave of him.
He granted it, and went his way,
Until ere vespers, late in the day,
He saw a maiden approaching
Who was both fair and charming,

Well-attired, most richly dressed.
The maiden greeted him, I attest,
Both prudently and courteously.
'Health and happiness, fair lady,
May God grant you!' he replied.'
'My house, sire,' next, she cried,
'Is all prepared to welcome you,
If you'll accept my gift to you
And welcome such hospitality;
You may stay, if you lie with me,
Such is my offer, and my intent.'
Not a few would have been content,
To thank her then five hundred fold,
But he towards the maid proved cold
For now he responded otherwise.
'Maiden, I thank you,' he replied,
'For the lodging, and hold it dear,
But to lie there with you, I fear,
Though it please, I shall not do.
'That or nothing, I offer you,'
She answered, 'by my two eyes.'
Then, unwilling to act otherwise,
He consented to what she wished,
Though his heart rebelled at this;
Reluctance now, yet unhappiness
He'll know later and great distress,
And she'll have much travail and pain,
The maid, who to lead him on is fain,
For she may find she loves him so
That she's unwilling to let him go.
Now as soon as he'd granted her
All she wished at her good pleasure,
She led him on to a strong bailey,
None fairer from there to Thessaly,
Which was enclosed all around

By a high wall and a moat profound;
And there was not another there
Except the knight, now in her care.

LINES 983-1042 THE KNIGHT OF THE CART
DINES WITH A MAIDEN

HERE had been set for her delight
Many a handsome room and bright,
With a great hall, spacious and fair.
Thus, riding along the river there,
They came to the maiden's tower,
Where the drawbridge was lowered,
To allow passage to them both.
So over they ride, nothing loath.
Here the great hall they discover
That is all roofed with tiles over.
They passed through the open door,
And there a table they saw before
Them, covered with a broad white
Cloth, all the dishes laid aright,
And about the table their eyes met
Tall candlesticks with candles set,
And there were cups of silver-gilt,
And two jugs of wine, one filled
With red, and the other with white.
Beside, on a bench-end, the knight
Espied two basins of warm water,
To wash their hands, on the other
End, a towel, finely worked, clean
And white, to wipe their hands, was seen.
Not one valet, servant or squire
Did he see, to work their desire;

And so, himself, the knight did take
The shield from his neck, and make
It all secure, by hanging it there,
On a hook, set true and square;
And then he placed his lance also
On a rack, with the shield below.
Then he dismounted from his steed
And went to help the maid but she
Had herself dismounted, with ease;
At which the knight was pleased,
That she cared not that he attend
On her, or help her to descend.
As soon as she touched the ground,
Without delay, she ran and found
A cloak of scarlet from her room,
And brought it to the knight whom
She then attired in the mantle.
The great hall was lit with candles
Though the stars above shone bright;
Tall twisted tapers shed their light.
Thus burning there, they lit the hall,
Clearly illuminating all.
About his neck she threw the cloak,
Then to him the maiden spoke:
'Friend,' she said, 'here is water
And a towel, with none to offer
Either but she whom you now see;
Wash your hands, and dine with me;
Here's food and drink for your pleasure,
So be seated at your leisure,
The hour demands it, as you see.'
He washed his hands, and willingly
Took his place, and there did bide
While she was seated at his side;
Then they ate and drank together
Until they rose, the meal over.

Lines 1043-1206 The Knight defends the maiden

WHEN they'd taken their last bite,
Said the maiden to the knight:
'Sir, feel free to roam outside;
No hurt to you is thus implied.
Remain alone there, if you will,
And wait there by yourself, until
You think that I must be abed.
Be you not troubled, as I said,
For you may then come to me,
If you would do as we agreed.'
'I'll keep my word,' replied the knight,
'And I shall, when the time is right,
Return, as you have asked me to.'
Then he retired, to admire the view
Outside, and waited in the court,
Until the time arrived, he thought,
To keep the promise he had made,
But found no trace of the maid
In the hall, on returning there;
No sign of his 'friend' anywhere.
Finding the maid nowhere in sight:
'Where'er she is,' declared the knight,
I shall seek her till I may find her.'
And straight he set out to discover
Her, bound as he was by his word.
Now, entering a room, he heard
A maiden uttering loud cries,
And hearing them he realised
Twas she with whom he must lie.
Then an open door he did spy

To a second room, and in full view,
Before his eyes, a knight there, who
Had overcome her, she half-naked
And held there helpless on the bed.
Then, trusting he came to her aid,
'Grant me succour!' cried the maid,
'Sir knight, who are now my guest,
If you should not this creature best
None other is there so to do;
He'll do me wrong in sight of you,
If you do not now rescue me;
For you it is must lie with me,
As you indeed have sworn to do.
Shall he before you, in plain view,
Impose his will on me by force?
Gentle knight, my sole recourse,
Grant me then succour, instantly!'
Our knight saw that most cruelly
The other held the maiden there,
For to the waist was she laid bare.
And he was angered and ashamed,
To see her naked to naked claimed,
Although he felt no jealousy;
If any was cuckold, twas not he.
Now at the doorway, armed aright,
Stood as guards, two tall knights,
And each man held a naked blade,
And behind them were displayed
Four men-at-arms each with an axe,
With which you might hew the back
Of a cow's carcase, cut it to suit,
As easily as you'd slice the root
Of a clump of broom or juniper.
He halted at the doorway there
And said: 'God, what am I to do?

'In full view Before his eyes,
a knight there, who Had overcome her'
The Romance of King Arthur and
his Knights of the Round Table (p214, 1917)
Sir Thomas Malory (15th cent), Arthur Rackham (1867-1939)
and Alfred William Pollard (1859-1944)
Internet Archive Book Images

Though committed elsewhere too,
In quest of the queen, Guinevere,
Yet to show the heart of a hare,
Does not befit me on such a quest.
If Cowardice doth my heart arrest,
And I should follow its command
I'll ne'er achieve what I've on hand.
Shame is mine if I here remain;
I feel for myself sheer disdain.
At even considering holding back,
My heart grows sad, my mind black;
I am so shamed and sore distressed,
I would gladly die, thus oppressed,
For having lingered here so long.
Not out of pride, for that were wrong,
Do I ask that God show me mercy,
For wishing to die here honourably
Rather than live a life of shame.
If this passage were free, this same,
What honour would I gain? Alas,
If they but gave me leave to pass
Without challenge, then indeed
The greatest coward, I concede,
That ever lived, would pass by.
And all the while I hear her cry
Calling for help continually;
Of my promise reminding me,
Heaping upon me dire reproach.'
So the doorway he did approach,
Thrusting in his head and shoulder.
Glancing upwards, entering further,
He saw two swords descend outright;
He drew backwards, but the knights
Could not check their blows' course.
They'd wielded their swords with force,

Such that both blades were the more
Damaged now as they struck the floor.
Seeing the blades break he was then
Less concerned by the four axe-men,
Fearing and dreading them no more;
For now he rushed towards all four,
Striking a guard and then another
In the side, and jostling those nearer
With his shoulder and arm such that
Toppling both he knocked them flat;
Then the third guard missed his aim,
As the fourth, attempting the same
Stroke, struck him and his mantle tore,
Cut his shirt, the white flesh scored,
So that from his shoulder he found
A stream of blood flowed to the ground.
Yet he still fought without restraint,
Of his wound making no complaint,
Pressing again more vigorously now,
Till he struck right upon the brow
Of him who was forcing his hostess.
He wished that now in her distress
He might fulfil his promise to her.
He dragged the man upright further,
Whether he would or no; but he
Whose aim had failed, suddenly
Came at him, to repeat his blow,
Hoping with his axe-blade so
To strike him as to split his head;
Yet he, defending himself instead,
Thrust the first foe at the other,
So that the axe, in its encounter,
Where the neck and shoulder meet
Cleft the one from the other complete.
Then our knight he seized the axe,

From the guard who'd just attacked,
And let go of the man he still held,
Since to defend himself seemed well;
The knights from the doorway again
Attacking him, with the three axemen,
And assailing him most cruelly.
To save himself he leapt promptly
Between the bed there and the wall,
And cried aloud: 'Now, come you all!
For if you were five and thirty yet,
To receive you I am now well set,
And you'll meet with battle enough;
I'll not be beaten by such poor stuff.'
But the maid who gazed at him said:
'By my eyes, you need have no dread
Of all such in future where I may be.'
And she dismissed, immediately,
All the knights and men-at-arms,
And they retired, free of more alarms,
Raising no objection, without delay.
While she took it upon herself to say:
'Sir, you have defended me bravely
Against all my household company;
Come now, and I'll lead you, withal.'
Hand in hand, they entered the hall,
Yet, as to her, he felt no pleasure,
Though set to enjoy her at leisure.

LINES 1207-1292 THE KNIGHT RESISTS THE MAIDEN

A bed was there, amidst the hall,
Its sheets were not disturbed at all,
But broad and white, and covered o'er;

Nor was this bed a thing of straw,
Nor with coarser fabrics spread;
A twin coverlet of silk instead,
Upon its mattress had been laid.
Down upon it now lays the maid,
But without shedding her chemise,
While he is scarcely at his ease
Untying and removing his hose,
Sweating to divest of his clothes;
Yet in the midst of his distress
His promise doth upon him press.
Whence is its power? Such its force
It urges and dictates his course,
Promise demands the debt be paid,
He must lie down beside the maid.
So down he lies now without delay,
But does not his naked form display,
Retaining his shirt as had she.
Nor does he touch her carelessly,
But keeps afar, and turns away,
Not a word to her doth he say
Like a novice forbidden speech,
Once he his own cot doth reach.
Nor does he turn on her his gaze,
Nor look towards her in any way.
He can show her not one courtesy.
Why? His heart's not moved you see.
She was gentle indeed and fair,
But not everything gentle and fair
Pleases everyone equally.
The heart he possessed was not free,
He had but one heart, and moreover
It was commanded by another.
He could not bestow it elsewhere.
Love, that has all hearts in its care,

Allows them all their proper place.
All? Only those in its good grace.
Who Love deigns to rule by law,
Ought to esteem himself the more.
Love so prized and esteemed his heart
It thus constrained him; for his part,
He was so proud of Love's decree,
I could not blame him certainly
For spurning what Love did not wish,
Holding to what he should cherish;
While the maid could clearly see
He was averse to her company,
Nor would he suffer it willingly,
And, having no desire to be
With her, would not seek to please her.
'If it would not displease you, sir,'
She said, 'I'll leave you here, and I
Will go to my own bed by and by,
So that you will be more at ease,
For I believe they cannot please,
My company, my society.
Do not think it a treachery,
If I but tell you what I feel;
And now let sleep upon you steal,
For you have so kept your promise,
That there is nothing more I'd wish
To ask of you, nor have the right.
I commend you to God, sir knight,
And thus I go.' So doth she leave,
Nor at their parting does he grieve,
But lets her leave him, willingly,
As one committed previously
To another; as the maid well sees,
And knows thus the thing must be.
So to her room she went instead,

Retiring, full naked, to her bed,
And there to herself she mused:
'Of all the knights I ever knew,
I know not one, compared to him,
Worth the third part of an angevin;
I see he pursues some great affair,
Graver than knight did ever dare,
And, equally, far more perilous.
God grant he return victorious!'
Then, falling asleep, she slept on
Till the sun shone clear at dawn.

Lines 1293-1368 The Knight and the maiden ride out together

As soon as it was day, then she,
Rose and dressed immediately.
And the knight, he too awoke,
Dressed himself, and donned his cloak,
And armed himself, without aid.
And soon there arrived the maid
Who saw he was already dressed.
'May this day prove of the best,'
She said, on seeing him, 'for you.'
'And for you may it prove so too,'
Answered the knight, for his part,
Adding that he would make a start
If but his horse be brought outside.
The maiden now called up his ride,
And said: 'Sir, I would travel today,
Awhile with you, along the way,
If you'd escort me beside you
And so conduct me according to

The custom and usage I once knew
Before we were held in Logres.'
(This custom, these privileges
Were such that a knight, at that day,
Meeting a lone maid, on his way,
Would no more mistreat the same
Nor dishonour her, if he his fame
Would maintain as a man of note,
Than he would seek to cut his throat.
If he treated her ill in short,
He'd be shunned in every court.
But if, on the way, another knight
Challenged him to stand and fight,
And then by arms fairly won her
The latter could then do with her
As he wished, and without shame,
Or attracting an ounce of blame.)
That is the reason that the maid
Said that she'd go with him that day,
If he was brave enough and would,
According to custom, be so good,
As to protect her from all harm.
And he replied: 'Have no alarm,
None shall offend, I promise you,
Without he first pay me his due.'
'Then I will go with you,' she said.
She ordered her palfrey to be led
To her, saddled, and it was done.
Her palfrey was brought at once,
And his war-horse to the knight,
Then they both mounted outright,
Without aid, and they rode away.
She spoke to him, but he no way
Cared for aught that she offered,
And not one word did he proffer.

Thought pleased him, words did not.
Oft Love re-opened, if he forgot,
The wound that it had dealt before,
Yet for neither comfort nor cure
Did he seek to address his wound,
Having no wish to ease his wound,
Nor seek a doctor or any balm,
Should it do him no greater harm,
But one whom he'd seek willingly.
Thus they took their way directly,
By roads and tracks, in the main,
Until they arrived at a fountain.
The fountain, set amidst a meadow,
Fell to a stone basin below,
And on the stone, we must assume,
Someone had left, I know not whom,
A comb of ivory inlaid with gold,
Such as never, since days of old,
Was seen by the foolish or the wise;
And wound in its teeth there lies
Almost half a handful of hair
Left by her who'd used it there.

LINES 1369-1552 THE FOUNTAIN, THE COMB,
AND THE TRESSES OF HAIR

WHEN the maiden, and she alone,
Saw the fount and basin of stone,
She, not wishing the knight to see,
Then took another path, hurriedly;
While, lost in his thoughts, the knight,
Who in his thoughts did much delight,
Did not at once perceive that she

Had turned aside, misleadingly;
But once the turn he did perceive,
Thought it designed to deceive,
And that she had turned aside
From the path they both did ride
To escape some danger there.
'Maiden, 'he cried, 'now beware,
You go astray; the way lies here;
For none do go aright, I fear,
Who from the true road depart.'
'Sir, on the better path we start,'
Said the maiden, 'so I believe.'
He replied: 'What you conceive,
My maid, to me is less than clear,
But plain enough I see that here,
Before me, lies the beaten way,
And, having come thus far, I say
I will not take some other road;
Take with me the path we rode,
For to this path I shall adhere.'
So they advanced till they came near
The stone, and now the comb he saw.
'I cannot,' said the knight, 'I'm sure,
Remember seeing, far or near,
So fine a comb as I see here.'
'Hand it' the maiden said, 'to me.'
And he replied: 'Most willingly.'
Then he bent, and took the comb.
As he held it, his gaze did roam
Over the hair entwined, awhile,
At which the maid began to smile.
Seeing this, he begged her to say
Why she smiled in such a way.
And she replied: 'Be silent, now,
For I shall tell you naught, I vow.'

'Why?' said he, 'Because I choose.'
He, on hearing her thus refuse,
Conjured her, as a believer
In lover staying true to lover,
Each he to she, and she to he:
'If you, 'he says, 'a lover be,
My maid, by that I conjure you,
And beg, and implore you too,
Hide not the reason then from me.'
'You press me so hard,' said she,
Indeed you cannot be denied,
I'll tell you all and nothing hide.
This comb, if I know nothing more,
It was the queen's, I am full sure.
And this, I say, you may believe,
That those strands of hair you see,
So fine and radiant and bright,
Woven in the teeth, sir knight,
The queen's head itself has owned,
They in no other place have grown.'
'By my faith,' the knight replied,
'Here many a king and queen abide,
Whom do you speak of, which queen?'
And she said: 'By my faith, I mean
King Arthur's wife, for it is she.'
When he heard this he could barely
Keep from bowing his head low,
Bending towards his saddle-bow.
Seeing his feelings thus displayed,
She wondered at him, for the maid
Fearing the consequence of all,
Thought him now about to fall.
If she was afraid, blame her not,
For he might swoon she thought.
And that were true, for so he might

So near to swooning was the knight;
For in his heart he felt such grief,
His colour paled, his power of speech
Was for a long while suspended.
The maiden quickly descended,
And ran as swiftly as any maid
To support him and bring him aid;
Not for anything would she seek
To see him fall there at her feet.
On seeing her, the knight felt shame,
And wishing to know why she came
To his aid, said: 'What need is here?'
Do not think she confessed her fear
Or told him the why and wherefore.
For it would have brought him more
Shame and anguish had she spoken,
And grieved him more than a token,
If she'd confessed the truth indeed,
So she concealed it tactfully:
'I descended to seek the comb,
Sir, for that reason have I come,
No more delay could I stand
Before I held it in my hand.'
And he who wished her to have
The comb gave it her now, save
That he first drew forth the hair.
Never did human eye, I declare,
See anything receive such honour;
For he commenced then to gather
It to him, so he might adore
The hair a hundred times and more,
Touching it to lips, eyes and brow;
Showing such joy as hearts allow.
Happy he feels himself and wealthy.
He places the tresses now, gently,

Beneath his shirt against his heart.
He'd not exchange them for a cart
Filled with emeralds and rubies.
Nor does he fear now that he
Will be afflicted with sores and pains;
Ground gems and pearls he disdains,
And the pleurisy and the leprosy,
For St. Jacques, St. Martin, has he
No need, he's such faith in her hair
He requires no other comfort there.
What did these tresses resemble?
If I say, you'll think I dissemble,
Or that I play the fool indeed.
When at the fair near St Denis
The stalls are full, riches galore,
By all of them he'd set no store
Unless he found those tresses there,
In proven truth, that shining hair.
And if of me the truth you'd find,
Then gold a hundred times refined,
And then as many more, its light
Would prove darker than the night
When tis compared to brightest day,
The brightest of the year, I say,
If beside the gold you set that hair,
And one with another did compare.
But why should I the tale prolong?
The maid remounted before long,
With the comb, while the knight
Transported was, in sheer delight
At bearing the tresses at his breast.
Leaving the plain they progressed
Through a forest, without delay,
Until they came to a narrow way,
Where one must ride after another,
It being impossible to do other,

Since two could not ride abreast.
The maid rode ahead of her guest,
Swiftly along this straight row,
And where it was most narrow,
They saw a knight approaching.
The maiden at once recognising
Him, when she saw him nearer,
Turned to the knight behind her
And said: 'Sir knight, do you see
This man who approaches swiftly,
All armed and ready for the fray?
He will hope to lead me away
With him, thinking me defenceless.
For his intentions I can guess;
He loves me, though tis all unwise,
He sends me messages and tries
To woo me, and long has done.
But my love's not for such a one,
I could not take him as my lover;
So help me God, I would rather
Die than on him bestow my love.
I do not doubt that joy doth move
Him now, and he feels great delight
As if he already owns me outright;
Yet now shall I see what you can do,
And you may show your bravery too;
Then shall I see, and you may show
That you can protect me from woe.
If you can guarantee my safety
Then I'll proclaim, and truthfully,
That you are right noble and brave.'
And he replied: 'On! And no delay!'
And that was as much as to say:
'At nothing need you feel dismay,
For little am I concerned at all
By these words that on me do call.'

LINES 1553-1660 THE KNIGHT OF THE CART
CHAMPIONS THE MAIDEN

WHILE they rode on conversing so,
The other knight advanced also;
He was alone, and riding swiftly
So as to meet with them directly;
All the more eager to make haste,
Thinking not the chance to waste;
By his own good fortune moved,
On seeing her whom he so loved.
As soon as he comes closer to her,
With heartfelt words he greets her,
Saying: 'May she I most long for,
Though grief not joy cometh before,
Be most welcome, where'er come from!'
Tis not fitting that she play dumb,
Given the warmth of his greeting,
Or be tardy in replying,
To his welcome with her tongue.
The knight though is done no wrong,
By her saluting him aright
For indeed her words are light,
Nor does the effort cost her aught.
Yet had he victoriously fought
In some joust or tournament
He'd not have felt, at that moment,
Worthier, nor could have found
More honour there or more renown.
Feeling his own self-worth regained,
He seized her horse's bridle-rein,
Saying: 'Now I shall lead you away;

For I've sailed well and true this day,
To reach so fine a harbour here.
My troubles are at an end, tis clear:
From danger have I come to port,
From sorrow to the joy I sought,
From great ill to perfect health,
Now have I my wish, my wealth,
Finding your state such as I see,
Where I may lead you on with me,
At once, without your saying no.'
She replied: 'Naught tells you so,
For this knight is escorting me.'
'He'll prove of little worth to be,'
He said, 'when I lead you away.
Sooner a peck of salt, or three,
He might eat, this knight, I see,
Than defend you now from me.
No knight there is, in my view,
From whom I would not win you.
Finding you here so opportunely,
Despite what he may do to thwart me,
I'll lead you off, before his eyes,
While his every effort I despise.'
The Knight of the Cart ignored
This show of pride, voiced abroad,
But, without boast or impudence,
Challenged him, in her defence,
Saying: 'Be not, sir, in such haste,
Nor your words so lightly waste,
But speak a little more reasonably;
For I shall not deprive you, I see,
Of any right, in her, you possess.
In my care and protection, no less,
The maid is here, so do no wrong;
Leave her, for you hold her too long;

She is not yet under your protection.'
The other knight gives him direction
To burn him, if he take her not despite
Him, but he replies: 'No, sir knight;
It would not be well if I so allowed.
I would prefer to fight you, I vow.
Yet, indeed, if we wish to fight,
Here we cannot do so aright,
In this narrow road, I maintain.
Let us go to some place again,
Wide enough, an open field or
Meadow.' He demands no more,
The knight replies: 'Most certainly,
You are not wrong, for I agree
This place is too narrow, I fear;
My steed is so hampered here,
That ere I can make him wheel
His flanks will be crushed I feel.'
Then, in much distress, he wheeled,
Though his steed no hurt revealed,
Nor was it harmed in any manner,
And said: 'Indeed, it doth me anger
That no better a place can we muster
For our fight, nor be seen by others,
For I'd wish all to understand
Which of us is the better man.
But come now, let us make haste,
And we'll find near to this place
Somewhere wide open and clear.'
Thus they came to a meadow near:
And this meadow was full of girls,
A host of knights and demoiselles,
Who that pleasant place employed
For the diverse games they enjoyed.
Nor were their games mere emptiness,

Some played backgammon, some chess,
While others played dice, happily;
Plus poins, hazard, and passe-dix.
Most of the folk played at these,
But others there they took their ease
Reliving their childhood joyfully;
Danced roundels, caroles, merrily,
Sang, and tumbled, leapt in the air,
Or wrestled each other, pair by pair.

LINES 1661-1840 A FATHER'S COMMAND AVOIDS AN IMMEDIATE ENCOUNTER

ON the far side of the green
An elderly knight could be seen,
Mounted upon a Spanish sorrel;
Golden were his saddle and bridle,
And his hair was tinged with grey.
One hand rested, with easy grace
At his side; in shirt-sleeves was he,
Since the day was clear and lovely,
Watching the dances and the play.
Over his shoulders he did display
A fine mantle of scarlet and vair.
On the other side, by the path there,
Were twenty armed knights and three,
All mounted on good Irish steeds.
As soon as the newcomers appeared,
All ceased their play, as they neared,
And round the meadow cried loudly:
'Now yonder comes the knight, see,
Who was carried along in the cart!
Let none here their games restart,

While this knight is here among us;
Cursed be those who continue thus,
Cursed be those who seek to play
While he is in this meadow today.'
Meanwhile the other knight, he
Who loved the maiden loyally,
And held her to be his delight,
Being son to the elderly knight,
Approached his father and said:
'Sire, I have won great happiness,
Who would hear me, hear now,
For God has given me, I vow,
All I wish, nor were it a greater
Gift if He had crowned me here,
No greater thanks would I owe,
Nor greater gain would I show,
For what I gain is good and fair.'
'I know not if tis thine, I swear,'
Said the noble father to his son.
Swiftly the knight replied in one:
'You know not? Can you not see?
Before God, Sire, doubt not me,
While you can see I hold her fast.
In the wood through which I passed
I met with her now, on the way.
I think God led her there today,
And I have taken her for my own.'
'I know not that he will condone
Such, who follows after you now;
He'll challenge you, I do avow.'
While they spoke all were pleased
To listen, for the games had ceased
On the instant our knight arrived,
All pleasure and gaiety had died,
Due to their scorn and enmity.

But the knight of the cart swiftly
After the maid now did follow,
Saying: 'Knight, let the maid go,
She to whom you have no right!
If you're brave enough, I'll fight,
And I will defend her from you.'
Then the elderly knight spoke too:
'Did I not claim it would prove so?
Fair son, now let the maiden go,
No longer seek her to detain.'
His son, displeased, is not fain
To do so; he swears he will not,
Saying: 'May God to this my lot
Deny all joy, if I yield her though!
I have her and will hold her so,
As a thing that is bound to me.
Every strap of my shield shall be
Severed, and it be torn away
And I must lose all faith, I say,
In my arms, and in my defence,
My lance and sword, and my strength,
Before I will yield the one I love.'
His father replied: 'I'll not approve
Such an encounter, nonetheless.
You trust too much in your prowess;
Instead, do now as I command.'
'Am I a child, who at your demand,
Should be filled with fear? Nay, with pride
Rather, I should boast,' he replied,
'That there's no knight, from sea to sea,
Where'er within this land may be,
Strong enough that I'd e'er yield her;
Not one whom I would fail, I aver,
To defeat, and in no short order.'
'I know, dear son' said his father,

'That this you do believe; indeed
You trust your powers, I concede,
And yet I would not wish this day
To see you thus attempt the fray.'
'I would be shamed, so I avow,
'Were I to accept your counsel now,'
His son replied. 'For cursed be he
Who doth; such must a recreant be
On account of you, nor seek to win.
Tis true we fare ill among our kin;
A better bargain I could make
With some stranger, and no mistake.
I swear that in some other place
I'd be received with better grace.
None who were unknown to me
Would thwart my will to this degree,
Yet here is annoyance and torment,
And great, therefore, my discontent
That you would find fault with me;
Yet he who finds fault so readily
Will ne'er bring a man to shame,
Merely his will the more inflame.
Should I not all my strength employ
In this, may God ne'er grant me joy,
But rather, in spite of you, I'll conquer.'
'I see,' said his father, 'by Saint Peter
'And the faith I hold in him, that my
Advice is worth nothing in your eyes,
And I'd waste my time rebuking you.
But I shall summon up means anew
Such that, despite what you desire
Yet will you do all I require,
And will submit to my command.'
Straight away he summoned a band
Of stalwart knights; it being done,

He ordered them to detain his son,
Whom he would see safe and sound.
And said: 'I shall have him bound,
Rather than he be allowed to fight;
You here are my band of knights,
Who owe me love and loyalty;
By the lands you hold from me,
I have summoned you to my side.
My son appears drunk with pride,
Half-mad indeed it seems to me,
He scorns to behave respectfully.'
They reply they will handle him,
Nor while they have charge of him
Will they allow the son to fight,
And he shall renounce outright,
Despite his wishes, the fair maiden.
They seized him, as they were bidden,
Gripping him by neck and shoulder.
'Do you not think', said his father,
'Yourself a fool now? Confess tis true,
Your strength proves little use to you,
You lack the power to joust or fight,
However difficult it might
Be, or painful, to say tis so.
You will be wise to do also
What pleases me and I desire.
Do you not know what I require?
So as to lessen your frustration
We'll follow, if tis your inclination,
This knight, today and tomorrow,
Through every last grove and hollow,
And each well-mounted, you and I.
We may perhaps at length descry
From his bearing and character,
That I would be right to concur,

And let you fight him as you wish.'
His son felt bound to accept all this,
Despite himself; like one who must
Accept whatever he can't adjust,
He said that he would suffer it so,
Provided that both of them did go.
When the folk in the meadow knew
Of the adventure both had in view,
They said: 'See how, by some art,
He who was mounted on that cart
Has gained such honour here today
That this maiden he leads away,
The friend of the son of my lord,
And my lord allows it. Be assured,
He must find some worth in him now
That this departure he doth allow.
Yet him a hundred times cursed be
Who halts his sport for such as he!
Play on.' And they began once more
Their games and dances, as before.

LINES 1841-1966 THE MARBLE TOMB

THEREUPON the knight of the cart
Turned, and prepared to depart,
For in the mead he would not stay,
And thus he led the maid away.
Swiftly, at full speed, they rode,
The father and son both followed.
Through the mown fields they went,
Till, with mid-afternoon's advent,
They came upon a place full fair,
A church, and by the chancel there

A graveyard bordered by a wall.
Circumspect, respectful in all,
The knight into the church went;
To pray to God twas his intent;
While the maiden held his horse,
Until his return in due course.
When he had made his prayer,
And while returning to her there,
An aged monk thus met his eyes
Who'd come upon him likewise.
As they met, the knight politely
Asked what that place might be
Since to him twas all unknown.
The monk said that the wall of stone
Enclosed a graveyard; he replied:
'So help you God, show me inside.'
'Willingly, sir,' the old monk said.
And, the monk going on ahead,
Entering, he saw the finest tombs
You'd find as far as Pampelune,
Or Dombes, and letters there were cut
On every tomb, at head and foot,
Giving the names of those who'd lie
Within the tombs there, by and by.
And he himself began to read
The names in order, so decreed,
And found: 'Herein will lie Gawain',
And here 'Louis', and there 'Yvain'.
And, after these three, thus the names
Of many another dear and famed
Knight, the most prized, and the best
Of this land, and of all the rest.
Among the others, one he found
Of marble, among those around
New, richer, finer than them all.

The knight then to the monk did call,
Saying: 'What purpose do they serve,
These tombs, here?' The monk observed:
'You have viewed the writing there;
If you've deciphered it with care
What's written there you'll recognise,
And what each tomb thus signifies.'
'The largest of them, long and wide,
What is its meaning?' He replied,
'I'll tell you truthfully, that tomb,
'So large the ground it doth consume,
Surpasses every other made,
So richly carved, and so arrayed,
None other finer can be shown;
Inside and out tis fine, you'll own.
Yet none of that is your concern,
Tis naught to you, as I discern;
For you shall never see inside.
Seven huge strong men, at its side,
Would be needed to lift the lid,
If to ope it any man would bid.'
For that lid is of heavy stone,
And to raise it, I'll make known,
Seven strong men it would need,
Stronger than you or I, indeed.
And there are letters written there:
"Who lifts this stone," they declare,
"And that solely by his own strength,
Will free all those women and men
Who are imprisoned in this land,
Of whom nor slave nor nobleman
Who is not born of this country
Can escape from their captivity;
All strangers are imprisoned so,
While natives they may come and go,

In and out, however they please.'"
The knight of the cart now seized
The stone, and raised it easily,
As if it weighed naught to such as he,
More readily indeed than any ten
Men might do, being thus bidden.
The monk was utterly amazed,
And nearly stumbled as if dazed,
In bearing witness to this marvel;
For he had ne'er seen aught to equal
This wonder all his days before.
He cried: 'Good sir, I do implore
You to reveal your name to me;
Will you disclose it?' 'No, truly,
I'faith, I will not,' said the knight.
'That saddens me, for if you might,'
The monk said, ''twere a courtesy,
And you some benefit might see.
Who are you now, and from whence
Do you come, and travel thence?'
'I am a knight, as you can see,
The realm of Logres my country,
And such is all I choose to say;
But you, for your part, tell me pray,
Who within this tomb shall lie?'
'Sire, he who liberates, say I,
All held in this realm in prison,
From which escape there is none.'
When his tale was done and ended,
The knight right promptly commended
The monk to God and all his saints,
Feeling, thus free of all constraint,
He might return now to the maid;
While the aged monk then made
To escort him from the church.

He thought to resume his search,
And, while the maiden mounted,
The monk, at her side, recounted,
Faithfully what the knight had done
Within, praying her, if twas known,
To tell him the knight's true name;
Yet, she replied, of that very same
She had no knowledge, but one thing
She, indeed, could say concerning
Him: where'er the wind did blow
None such as he did come and go.

LINES 1967-2022 THE FATHER AND SON, AND THE MAID, DEPART

OF the monk the maid takes leave
And after her the knight doth weave.
Now arrive the father and son,
Following after, who see the monk,
Standing beside the church alone.
The aged knight, in courteous tone,
Asks: 'Sir, tell us now, if you might,
If you, perchance, have seen a knight,
Accompanied by a maid, go by?'
'I'll not be loath,' is his reply,
To tell you all that I have seen,
For they not long ago have been
Where you are; the knight, within,
Performed so wondrous a thing
As to raise high the lid of stone,
That tops the marble tomb, alone,
Without the slightest sign of strain.
He's gone to seek the queen, again,

And he will doubtless rescue her
And, with her, all the others there.
That twill be so, to you is known,
For you have read upon the stone
The letters that are written there.
There was never knight, I swear,
Born of woman, who sat a steed
Was equal to this knight indeed.'
Then turned the father to his son:
'How seems it now? Is he not one
Full worthy who performs this feat?
Who's in the wrong you may see:
You well know if twas you or I,
I'd not have you fight this knight,
For all the city of Amiens;
And yet you'd struggle on and on
Before relinquishing your aim.
We may as well return again,
For great folly it would be
To follow him, it seems to me.'
His son conceded: 'I do agree:
To follow would be vanity.
If it so please you, let us go!'
And wise they were in doing so.
Meanwhile the maid doth ride
Close by the knight's left side,
Striving to make him heed her,
Seeking his name to discover;
She asks him to speak it plain,
Begging him, time and time again,
Till, all annoyed, he answers her
'Have I not but now made it clear,
Of Arthur's realm I am, no less?
I swear, by God and his goodness,
That my name you'll never know!'

She bids him give her leave to go,
That she might thus return, and he
Grants her request right willingly.

LINES 2023-2198 THE KNIGHT OF THE CART
ACQUIRES NEW COMPANIONS

THEREON the maiden did depart,
While till late the Knight of the Cart
Rode on, free of her company.
After vespers, near compline, he
Saw, as he his road pursued,
A knight approaching, who issued
From the hunt in a wood nearby.
His helmet-mail was all untied,
And on a great steed he did ride
To which the venison was tied,
That God had granted him to take.
The hunter swift his way did make
Towards the knight, to whom he
Now offered hospitality:
'Night,' he said, 'will soon be here;
Time to seek lodgings that is clear,
And you being here upon my land
I have a house quite near to hand,
To which I thus might lead you now.
None has lodged you better, I vow,
Than I have the power to do;
I'd be pleased, if it pleases you.'
'I should be pleased indeed,' said he,
So his host, immediately,
Sent his son ahead to prepare
The house, and devote all his care

To making sure supper was ready.
Without delay, the lad gladly
Ran to execute his command.
Right willingly he set on hand
The preparations, while the rest
Followed on, host, maid and guest,
Wending their way, all leisurely,
Till the host's house they did see.
The host it seems shared his life
With a most accomplished wife,
And five sons he held most dear,
Two were knights it would appear,
And two daughters, noble and fair,
Who were maids, still in his care.
None of them were native-born,
But were from their country torn,
And held in durance many a year,
For they were prisoners of fear,
Who hailed from the realm of Logres.
When his host, at his own request,
Had led the knight into his court,
His lady ran out to meet her lord
And all his sons and daughters too,
Vying in their efforts to do
The guest honour, on their account,
Greet him, and help him to dismount.
His five sons and his daughters
Gave scant attention to their father,
Knowing that such was as he wished.
But warmly they honoured their guest.
Once they'd eased him of his armour,
One of his host's fair daughters
Draped a mantle about his shoulder
That did her own shoulders cover.
I need not say that, at supper, he

Was served well and fulsomely;
And when the meal was at an end
They showed no hesitation then
In speaking of matters various.
Firstly, his host proved curious
As to the knight's own origin,
His land, and with that did begin,
Yet he asked not after his name.
The knight responded to this same:
'From the realm of Logres am I,
And never before have cast an eye
Upon this land.' And when his host
Heard this, then he did appear most
Troubled and worried for his guest,
His wife, and children too, distressed.
For then indeed, his host did say:
'Woe that you came here, this day,
Fair sir, trouble will come to you!
For, like ourselves, to servitude
And exile you will be reduced.'
Said the knight: 'Then, whence come you?'
'From your land, sir, we have come,
And, of that land, is many a one
Now imprisoned in this country.
Accursed may such customs be,
And those who do them maintain!
For here no stranger ever came
Who was not forced to remain,
Whom this country did not detain.
Who so wishes may enter here,
But must remain, year upon year.
Of you own fate you may be sure:
Doubtless, you'll depart no more.'
'Be sure I will,' the knight replied,
'If I can,' but his host now sighed:

'What? You think to depart still?'
'Yes, if it should be God's will;
And I do all within my power.'
'Well then, at that very same hour
All the others would be set free,
For when one man genuinely
Issues forth from out this prison,
All the others without question
Unchallenged, may do the same.'
Then the knight's host explained
That he indeed had heard it said
That a great knight, to virtue bred,
Had made his way into that land,
Seeking the queen, whom Meleagant,
The king's son, had there detained;
And said to himself: 'I do maintain
That this is he, and will tell him so.'
So said: 'Hide not from me, though,
Sire, aught of your purpose here,
On the understanding, be you clear,
I'll give you the best advice I can.
I myself will gain, you understand,
If you indeed achieve success.
Tell me the truth,' he begged his guest,
'For your own benefit and mine.
I think you have come, by design,
Into this land to seek the queen,
Among these heathen folk, I mean,
Who are far worse than Saracens.'
And the knight answered him again:
'I came here for no other reason.
I know not where my lady's prison
Might be, but I would rescue her.
Good advice I lack, in this affair;
Give me wise counsel if you can.'

His host replied: 'You have on hand
A grievous task, sire, for the way
You travel will take you, this day,
Straight to the Bridge of the Sword.
Advice you need, of that I'm sure:
If thus my counsel you will take,
To that bridge your way you'll make
By a more certain path, and fair,
And I'll see you escorted there.'
He who the most direct path sought:
Then asked: 'Is that road as short
As the other way that I may go?'
And his host answered him: 'No,
The path is longer, but it is sure.'
And he said: 'Tell me no more
Of it, then, but instruct me now
In that other which I will follow.'
'Sir, truly there you shall fare ill:
If to take the other path you will,
Tomorrow you will reach a pass
Where you'll find sorrow, alas;
Its name is: The Pass of Stones.
The troubles that passage owns
Would you that I told you now?
A horse's width it will allow,
Two men cannot go side by side;
So guarded is it, none can ride
There safely, and so well-defended.
Your journey may soon be ended
The moment you reach it; know
You will encounter many a blow
From lance and sword, and render
Many, before you travel yonder.'
Yet, when the host's tale was done,
His son then spoke, and he was one

Who was a knight, to this effect:
'If, father, you do not object,
With this lord now I shall go.'
And another of his sons arose
And cried: 'Then, I will go also.'
And the father gave leave to both,
Willingly yielding his consent.
Now, accompanied, as he went,
Our thankful knight would be,
Right pleased to have their company.

LINES 2199-2266 THE PASS OF STONES

THE conversation over, they led
The Knight of the Cart to his bed;
And he was glad to take his rest.
At daybreak he rose and dressed
As soon as ever it was light,
And the son who was a knight,
Rose also, as did his brother.
The two knights donned their armour,
Took their leave, while they were led
By the young brother who rode ahead,
And in company they took their way
Till to the Pass of Stones came they;
The hour of prime was close at hand.
A tower in the midst did stand,
Where was placed a man on guard.
As they approached it from afar,
He on the tower espied the three;
Seeing our knight, he cried, loudly:
'He comes for ill! He comes for ill!'
And then they saw, armed to the hilt

In bright armour, a mounted knight
From the tower come forth to fight,
And two servants, one either side,
Carrying axes, strode there beside.
And as the company neared the pass,
He who defended that crevasse
Reproached the Knight of the Cart:
Crying: 'Vassal, full bold thou art,
And foolish indeed must thou be
Thus to have entered this country.
No man should ever venture here
Who in that cart did e'er appear;
And may God ne'er grant him joy!'
Then both did their spurs employ,
And drove their steeds full hard,
And he who the pass did guard
Shattering his lance, at a stroke,
Let fall the remnants, as it broke;
While the other his lance did wield
To strike the neck above the shield,
Throwing his foe to the stones
Leaving him lying there to groan.
Then the axe-men at once up-rose
Yet sought not to land their blows,
Not wishing to harm him indeed,
Neither the knight, nor his steed.
And the knight perceiving that they
Declined to strike him in any way
Showing no wish to do him harm,
Drew not his sword nor gave alarm,
But passed on by them, full swiftly,
And, after him, his company.
And then the one axeman cried
To his fellow: 'No such knight
Have I seen, for he has no peer.

Wondrous tis what we saw here,
That a passage he made by force!'
'For God's sake, spur your horse,'
Cried his brother to the younger,
'And hasten on then to our father,
And tell him of all this adventure.'
But the lad swore he'd not venture
To carry the message back, not so,
He would not leave the knight to go,
Till that knight had dubbed him true,
And had rendered him a knight too.
Let him take the message and go,
If his brother cared about it so.

Lines 2267-2450 The Knights of Logres invade the Country

SO the three rode on together, there,
Till nearly nones, the time of prayer.
And, towards nones, they did see,
One who asked who they might be
And they answered: 'Knights, who fare
Here, busy about our own affairs.'
And the man said to the knight:
'Hospitality I offer this night
To you and all your company.'
This he said to the one that he
Took to be the lord and master,
Who replied: 'I seek no shelter
At this hour; for tis not right
That any man doth rest ere night
Or at his ease in comfort lies
When set on some great enterprise.

And such business I have on hand
As yet I stay not, you understand.'
And the man answered him thus:
'My house is not so near to us,
Some little distance tis away;
You would arrive at close of day
And find good lodging, as I state;
When you reach it, twould be late.'
'Then I'll go thither,' the knight said.
At which the man went on ahead,
Leading them on, along the road.
And, after him, the three knights rode.
And when they had gone some way,
They met a squire, while yet twas day,
Who was galloping along that road,
And the mount the squire bestrode
Was like an apple plump and round.
He to the man did warning sound:
'Sire, sire, come you on, in haste,
For those of Logres come against
This land, and all the people here,
And they commence a war, I fear;
Already there is battle and strife,
And they declare, upon my life,
A knight has entered this country
Who has been in battles a-plenty;
Nor can his passage be denied,
Wherever he wishes he will ride,
All let him pass, reluctantly.
They say that those in this country,
All who are captive, he will free;
While we shall endure captivity.
So take my counsel and make haste!'
Thus after him the man now raced.
But the three knights felt delight,

They were now eager for the fight,
Hearing this, and to aid their side.
And the elder son, he loudly cried:
'Sire, you heard what the squire said.
Let us then gallop on ahead,
And aid our people in their fight!'
Meanwhile the man had fled outright,
Never pausing, whilst heading for
A fortress high which rose secure
Upon a hill, well-fortified,
And to its gate did swiftly ride,
As after him the others pounded.
This high fortress was surrounded
By a great wall, and moat beside.
The moment they were all inside
A portcullis fell, at their heels,
That the passage-way did seal
Behind them, offering no escape.
'On, on!' they cried, 'in this scape
We must not linger.' On they rode
After the man, and at speed did go,
Till they came to where it ended,
An exit, which was undefended;
Yet as soon as the man was through
A portcullis appeared there too,
Closing the passage to the three.
They were much dismayed to see
Themselves caught in such a plight,
Thinking themselves enchanted quite.
But he of whom I shall say more
A ring upon his finger bore,
Whose stone was of such virtue
That those who held it in their view
Saw through all enchantment's lies.
He held the ring before his eyes

'*They saw, on exiting the tower*
A battle had begun that hour'
The Romance of King Arthur and
his Knights of the Round Table (p15, 1917)
Sir Thomas Malory (15th cent), Arthur Rackham (1867-1939)
and Alfred William Pollard (1859-1944)
Internet Archive Book Images

And, gazing at the stone, said he:
'Lady, ah, God help me, lady,
Of your aid have I great need;
If you can aid me now, indeed.'
This lady was of faery kind,
She had to him the ring assigned,
And cared for him from infancy.
In what place he e'er might be,
He had true confidence that she
Would bring him aid in misery;
Yet after gazing on the ring,
And upon his lady calling,
He knew enchantment was there none
And all was real that had been done,
And they shut in, and prisoned hard.
Yet they found there a postern barred,
A doorway, both low and narrow.
Drawing their swords together, lo,
They struck with the blades so hard,
All at once, they shattered the bar.
They saw, on exiting the tower
A battle had begun that hour,
In the meadows, fierce and hot,
And a thousand knights, God wot,
Fought on one side and the other,
Beside the mass of foot-soldiers.
While descending to the meadow,
Both wise and temperate did show
The elder son, who now did say:
'Ere entering the field this day,
It would be wise, I think, to know
By enquiry, which side below
Is ours, and where our people are.
I am not certain, but near or far
I will go wander, and ascertain.'

'Struck his head About the eye, and left him dead.'
The Blue Poetry Book (p106, 1891)
Andrew Lang (1844-1912), H. J. Ford (1860-1941)
and Lancelot Speed (1860-1931)
Internet Archive Book Images

'I wish you would so and again
Return to us, and that directly.'
Swiftly he went, returned as swiftly,
And said: 'Good fortune serves our turn,
For I was able to discern
These are our troops, on this side.'
Then the knight at once did ride
Straight into the thick of the fight,
Encountered an advancing knight,
Jousting with him, struck his head
About the eye, and left him dead.
Then the younger son dismounts
And seizes the dead man's mount;
Then the armour he doth possess,
Cladding himself with adroitness.
And once clad, he takes the field,
Mounting, grasps the dead man's shield,
The painted lance, strong, and heavy,
Straps the sword to his side swiftly,
A sharp blade, and gleaming bright,
Following his brother and the knight
Into the melee there obtaining;
His lord the knight maintaining
Himself right well for a great while,
Shattering, rending shields in style,
And bright helms, and coats of mail.
No wood or steel slowed his assail,
He left there, defenceless, instead,
Unhorsed, the wounded and the dead.
Unassisted, so well he wrought
That he discomfited all he fought,
While the brothers did as well as he,
Those two who kept him company.
The folk of Logres marvelled then
Not knowing him, and asked his men,

His host's sons, who he might be.
Such the demands, and: 'This is he,
Gentlemen,' they gave answer, 'who
Will end our exile, the misery too
Endured in this captivity,
Where we've long languished unfree;
Honour on him we should bestow
Since, to free us from prison so,
Many a peril he has passed
And many more shall, ere the last.
Much will he do and much has done.'
All were delighted now, bar none;
Upon hearing all that they said,
All rejoiced, thus the news spread,
Travelling so swiftly, all around,
Everywhere the word did sound,
Till all had heard and all men knew.
With all the joy that did ensue
Strength and courage rose anew,
And many an enemy they slew,
Working such great havoc there,
It seems to me, in that affair,
Because of one knight's deeds, rather
Than those of all the rest together.
And had nightfall not been so near
They'd have slain them all tis clear;
But night came on, and so dark a night
That they were forced to end the fight.

LINES 2451-2614 FRESH LODGINGS AND AN ENCOUNTER

THEN those defeated in the fight
They all pressed about the knight,

Gathering round him as he did ride,
Grasping his reins, on either side,
And thus they all began to choir:
'True welcome be to you, fair sire.'
Each saying: 'By my faith, sir knight,
You shall lodge with me tonight;
By God sir, by his holy name,
No other lodging shall you claim.'
What each says they all do say,
Wishing to lodge the knight that day,
Both the youngsters and the old,
Crying, a multitude all told:
'Better with me than lodge elsewhere.'
So each claimed, before him there,
And they, all jostling one another,
Sought to claim him from each other,
And, with that, almost came to blows.
Then he declared, to act like foes
Was great foolishness, pure folly.
'Now cease,' he cried, 'this rivalry,
That does no good to you or me.
Among us let no quarrelling be,
Rather go lend each other aid.
No outcry should you have made
In seeking to lodge me, instead
You should seek, as I have said,
To lodge me now in such a place
That all may benefit, then haste
Me thence upon the way I go.'
Then they all, as one, did bellow:
'At my house then! No, at mine!'
'Say nothing more, for I decline,'
Said the knight, 'and add no fuel,
For the wisest of you is a fool
To set yourself to arguing there.

You should advance my affairs,
Yet you seek to divert my aim.
If you have one and all the same
Intent concerning me in this,
To do me such honour and service,
As any man was ever shown,
Then I, by all the saints in Rome,
Could be no more obliged to you,
Than I am now, and do so express.
God give me health and happiness,
Your intentions please me as much
As if you each had shown me such
Kindness and honour here, indeed;
So let the wish stand for the deed.'
He appeases and woos them so;
Then to a knight's house they go
At their ease, to grant him lodging,
And there they all seek to serve him.
They do him honour and service,
Each deriving great joy in this,
All evening till bedtime is near,
For they all hold him most dear.
At dawn when it is time to leave
Each seeks to join his company,
Presents himself, and so offers,
But tis not his wish or pleasure,
That any man with him shall go,
Except the two sons of his host
Whom along with him he'd brought;
With them alone, the way he sought.
All that day, from early morning,
They rode on, until the evening,
Meeting not with any encounter.
Yet when issuing, however,
From a forest, galloping along,

A knight's manse they came upon,
His wife there, seated by the door,
Who seemed a fine lady and more.
And as soon as ever she did see
The approach of the knights three,
She arose from her seat to meet
The travellers, and them did greet,
With delight, saying: 'Welcome all!
Be pleased to enter now my hall;
Here is lodging, and so descend!'
'Lady, to your command we bend,
Descend we shall,' said the knight,
'Grateful to lodge here this night.'
They descended, and as they did
Their mounts were led as she bid
To the stables; here all was order.
Then she called her sons and daughters;
To her side swiftly they did run,
Handsome and courteous the sons,
And the daughters they were fair.
Then she bade the lads take care
To unsaddle and groom the steeds;
None would disobey her indeed,
But did good service willingly.
The knights they disarm all three,
The daughters assisting readily;
The armour removed, they swiftly
Bring them short mantles to wear,
Leading the three men, then and there,
Into the manse, full large and fine.
Its lord was absent at that time,
Out in the woods, and also there
Two of his sons with him did fare;
He soon returned, and all did run,
Being well-mannered every one,

To greet their master at the door.
The venison the three men bore
They soon removed and untied,
Crying the news to him, inside:
'Sire, sire, though you know it not yet,
Three fair knights have you for guests.'
'God be praised for that,' said he,
Then he and the two sons, all three
Glad welcome to their guests display;
All the household, without delay,
Even the least of them, prepared,
To perform their functions there.
Some seek to hurry the meal along,
Others light candles, and bring on
Towels and basins so as to offer
Their guests the use of clean water,
With which they might wash their hands,
As all do gladly where they stand.
Having washed, all take their seats,
Not one thing the hosts complete
Seems a trouble or burdensome.
But, as the meal begins, doth come
A knight who waits outside the door,
Prouder than a bull, equipped to gore,
Such being a most proud beast indeed;
For he sits there, upon his steed,
Fully armed from head to toe.
One foot is in the stirrup below,
The other foot is jauntily placed
Along his horse's neck with grace,
Thus adding to his careless air.
Behold, this knight advanced there,
Though none saw him or took note
Till he was before them, and spoke:
'Who is that man, I seek to know,

Who such pride and folly doth show,
Who possesses such an empty head
He comes to this land, being led
To cross o'er the Bridge of the Sword.
Yet all his effort shall be ignored,
And all his journey prove in vain.'
Then he, who felt for this disdain
No fear, with confidence replied:
'I'm he who o'er the Bridge would ride.'
'You? You? Dare you dream it so?
You should consider e'er you go,
Before you undertake this thing,
The end to which tis bound to bring
All this intent of yours and you,
And think on the memory too,
Of the cart on which you rode.
What pain you feel I cannot know
At how you were transported there,
But no wise man in this affair
Would dare now to show his face,
If he felt shame at such disgrace.'

LINES 2615-2690 THE KNIGHT OF THE CART
ACCEPTS A CHALLENGE

AT all that was said and heard,
He deigned not to say a word;
But the master of the mansion,
And the rest, with good reason,
Now openly expressed wonder,
'Ah, God, such misadventure!'
Each to himself said, inwardly,
'Now cursed be the hour, utterly,

That hateful cart was first conceived,
A vile thing was thus achieved.
Ah God, of what was he accused?
And by the cart was thus abused?
For what crime was he to blame?
All his days he'll bear the shame.
If of reproach he now were free
In all the world there could not be,
However his prowess were shown,
Such a knight, both seen and known,
To equal this knight now in merit.
Indeed, to tell the truth of it,
If all fine knights were compared
None were as noble or as fair.'
Thus all folk in common sighed.
But the newcomer, full of pride,
Recommenced that speech of his:
'Sir knight, now, who, hearing this,
To the Bridge of the Sword do go:
If you would cross the water so,
Most safely and most easily,
I'd have you do so, and swiftly,
For in a skiff you may ride.
But, when you reach the other side,
For that trip I'd have you pay,
And take your head then, I may,
Or hold you there at my mercy!'
Our knight replies he doth not seek
Any trouble or misadventure;
He his head will not so venture,
Nor risk the passage so, for aught.
To which the other makes retort:
'Since you will not have it so,
Whoever's be the shame and woe,
You must come forth, willingly,

And fight hand to hand with me.'
To content him, our knight said:
'If I could refuse, I would, instead,
Most willingly decline to fight,
But I would rather do what's right
Than be forced to commit a wrong.'
Rising from the table, ere long,
Where they were sitting, the knight then
Made request of the serving-men
To go, quickly, and saddle his steed,
And seek out his arms, with speed,
And bring to him his armour there.
They performed his orders with care;
One now saddled and brought his horse,
Another armed him and, in due course,
Mounted, fully armed, he appeared,
Know you, clad in his warlike gear,
Grasping his shield by the leathers,
Astride his steed, like one forever
Destined, to be, where'er men dare,
Counted among the brave and fair.
His steed seemed to be his alone,
It suited so, twas as if his own,
As seemed the shield he gripped, they said;
And the helmet, laced to his head,
Seemed to cleave to it so well
You'd have been hard put to tell,
That the helm might borrowed be;
For he'd have pleased you so that he
Was born to it, you'd have inferred.
For all this you may take my word.

'*They hew at helm and mail and shield*'
St. Nicholas [serial] (p44, 1873)
Mary Mapes Dodge (1830-1905)
Internet Archive Book Images

LINES 2691-2792 THE KNIGHT OF THE CART
DEFEATS HIS OPPONENT

OUTSIDE the gate, on open ground,
There is a fitting place to be found,
Where the encounter is to be.
As soon as they each other do see,
They meet each other full swiftly,
Coming together right furiously,
Dealing such blows with the lance,
The weapons break at their advance,
Flying to pieces, each splintering.
Then to their good swords retreating,
They hew at helm and mail and shield,
Slicing the wood, shearing the steel,
Dealing each other many a wound.
Such fell blows they land these two
Tis as if they've struck some pact;
While many a blow upon the back
Of one mount or the other falls,
Till the blades are wet with blood,
Bathing their flanks with a flood;
Such that of both steeds they dispose,
Each falling dead beneath their blows.
Once their feet are on the ground,
The knights upon each other round,
As if possessed by mortal hatred,
Their energy could not be bettered,
Wielding their swords most cruelly,
As often, and as recklessly,
As one who would his fortune make
At dice, will ever double his stake,

Whene'er he loses, and play on.
Yet this game proves a different one,
For here there's no loss or failure,
Only blows, and sharp encounter,
Fierce and cruel under the sun.
All had issued from the mansion,
Sire and lady, sons and daughters,
None remained, friend or other,
All the household standing there,
In line, to witness that affair,
Keen to see who might yield,
On that broad and level field.
Ashamed, the Knight of the Cart,
Fearful of seeming faint of heart,
Seeing his host there looking on,
And all the crowd gazing as one,
Standing close, in line together,
Feels his heart swell with anger,
Thinking he ought, full long ago,
Surely, to have felled this foe,
Who so engages him in combat.
He launches himself fiercely at,
The other; like a tempest dread,
Striking him full upon the head,
Pushing, pressing him so fiercely
He near dislodges him completely;
From his ground he drives his foe
Till the other's near exhausted, so
As to offer but slight defence.
Then he recalls the dire offence
His foe has committed at the start,
Shaming him concerning the cart.
So he assaults him and beats him
Till he's broken at the neck-brim
Every leather strap and tie,

Making the other's helmet fly
From his head, and his ventail.
Such is his foe's pain and travail,
That he is forced to cry for mercy,
Like to the lark that cannot flee,
Nor withstand the hawk's attack,
Since all protection it doth lack,
As its foe passes and surmounts it.
So, shamed, for his own benefit,
Must the knight at once beg for,
Mercy, since he can do no more.
When the Knight of the Cart heard
His plea, his blow he thus deferred,
And said: 'Mercy it is you'd seek?'
'This is no great wisdom you speak,'
Replied the other: 'a fool could see
I never wished for aught, woe's me,
As much as I wish for mercy now.'
Our Knight replied, 'Then, I avow,
That you must in the cart now ride;
Naught you may say upon your side
Counts aught for me if you do not
Mount the cart; let that be your lot,
And atone for all that so vilely your
Foolish lips have reproached me for.'
'May it please God I'll ne'er do so,'
Replied his defeated enemy. 'No?'
Said the knight, 'then you shall die.'
'Sire, you can kill me,' came reply,
'Yet for God's sake, I beg of you
Mercy, and only ask that you do
Not compel me to mount the cart,
There's naught I'll not accept, apart
From that, howe'er painful to me;
But a hundred times I'd rather be

Slain, than suffer such disgrace;
Naught else is there I would not face,
That, of your goodness and mercy,
You might choose to inflict on me.'

LINES 2793-2978 A MAIDEN SEEKS THE DEFEATED KNIGHT'S HEAD

WHILE the knight thus sought mercy,
The Knight of the Cart did perceive
A maid in the field, nearing, who
Rode upon a mule of dusky hue;
Her clothes dishevelled, head bare,
A whip grasped in her hand there,
She struck the mule mighty blows,
And ne'er a steed at full gallop goes
Faster, in truth, than did that mule
As she rushed on towards the duel.
'God give you joy and fill your heart,'
She cried, to the Knight of the Cart,
'With all that doth please, sir knight!'
And he, who heard her with delight,
And gladly gave ear to all she said,
Replied: 'God bless you, my maid,
And grant you good health and joy!'
Then she begged him for his employ:
'Sir knight,' she said, 'I, from afar,
Come, in great need, where you are,
To ask of you a favour, whose
Value to me and worth to you
Is as great as ever it could be,
And you will yet, I do foresee,
Have need of me in this affair.'

And he replied: 'Tell me, my fair,
What you wish then, and if I may
I'll grant it you, without delay,
Unless it should prove too dear.'
And she replied: ''Tis the head, here,
Of this knight that you do conquer.
For, truth to tell, you could never
Find a wretch so vile and faithless.
You'll do no wrong, I may confess,
No sin, but a goodness and charity;
For the most faithless there could be
Of all wretches in this world is he.'
Now when his defeated enemy
Heard that she desired his death:
'Believe her not! With every breath,
She breathes hatred of me,' he said,
'I beg that you show mercy, instead,
By that God at once Son and Father,
He who chose as His Son's Mother
His handmaiden and His daughter!'
'Ah, believe you not this traitor,
Good sir knight!' now cried the maid,
'May God grant you, all your days,
All you desire of joy and honour,
And grant you, in your endeavour,
All the success that might be won.'
And now the knight was so taken
With her words, he stood in thought
Perplexed, as to whether he ought
To grant her the head she desired,
Or if, by kindness and mercy fired,
He ought to take pity on his foe.
For regarding her, and him also,
He wishes to grant their demands;
Largesse and Pity both command

Him to do right toward these two,
For he is kind and generous too;
But if she bears the head away
Mercy and pity die that day;
And yet if she bear it not thence,
Largesse he cannot dispense.
So do both pity and largesse,
Hold him confined, and in distress,
Tormented, driven by each in turn.
The maiden for the head doth burn,
That she wishes him to grant her;
While his enemy, upon the other
Hand, seeks pity and kindness;
And since he has made request
For mercy, should not it be his?
Yes, for in such like case as this
Where he has felled an enemy,
And forced him to sue for mercy,
He's never failed to heed that cry,
Never such mercy has he denied,
Not once has he refused it ever,
Nor e'er born a grudge thereafter.
Surely he could not now be seen,
Since such his custom it has been,
To refuse a man the like request?
And should he grant, at her behest,
The head? Why yes, if he but could.
'Sir knight,' he said, 'now I would
That you should fight with me again,
And such mercy now, for your pains,
I shall indeed to you extend,
That you might your head defend,
As to grant you to arm your body,
And take your helm, and be ready.
As completely as e'er you might.

But if I conquer you, sir knight,
Once again, then you shall die.'
'No more I seek,' came the reply,
'Nor other mercy do I demand.
And I will fight thee as I stand,
And give thee the advantage that
I shall not move, for this combat,
From the place where I am now.'
He clads himself and, with a bow,
They return to the fight, eagerly.
Yet our knight conquered more swiftly,
After the mercy he'd rehearsed,
Than e'er he'd done at the first.
And thus, at once, the maid did cry:
'Spare the wretch not, now, say I,
Sir knight, whatever he may say!
If he had conquered you this day
He'd not have spared you at all.
If you believe words he lets fall,
Know he'll beguile you once more.
Cut off the head, and so be sure,
Of the most faithless man that we
Have in this land, and grant it me!
For, grant it me you ought, indeed,
Since I shall reward so fine a deed,
Full well, when the day shall arise,
While, if he can, with his vile lies,
He will beguile thee for your pains.'
The other seeing death close again,
Begged him for mercy, long and loud.
But his pleas prove worthless now,
Whatever words he seeks to say;
By the helm he's dragged away.
The leather straps no more avail,
The white coif, and the ventail,

From his head, away these fly;
While he doth loud, and louder, cry,
'Mercy, for God's sake, sire! Mercy!'
The knight replies: 'Full wise I'll be,
Having once granted you mercy,
No longer shall I show you pity.'
'Ah,' says he, 'now ill would it be
To heed her, who's my enemy,
And kill me in such a manner.'
While she who seeks the favour
Exhorts the Knight of the Cart
To sever his head, for her part,
And not trust a word of his lies.
He strikes, and away the head flies,
To the ground, doth the body fall;
Thus the maid is satisfied withal.
The Knight of the Cart then takes
The head by the hair, and makes
To give it to her, who of it has joy,
Who says: 'So may your heart enjoy
Joy as great, from your every wish,
As doth my own heart here in this,
All that I most have coveted.
By naught was my sorrow fed,
But that the man was still alive.
A boon, since for me you did strive,
You shall have at the proper hour;
For you shall gain for this favour
A worthy reward, I promise you.
Now I will go, commending you
To God, may He guard you from ill.'
And so the maiden departs at will,
As they to God commend each other.
But all of those who came together
To view the fight, of that country,

Now filled with joy at his victory,
At once relieve him of his armour,
In their joy, and show all honour
To him, in every way they can.
Once again they rinse their hands,
And take their places for a meal,
Happier than they were wont to feel,
And so they eat more joyfully still.
When at length they'd had their fill,
His host said to his honoured guest,
Seated by him, not among the rest:
'Twas long ago we came, I fear,
From the kingdom of Logres, here.
There were we born, thus we wish
That honour come to you in this
Country, and joy and fortune too,
For we would profit as much as you;
And twould profit many another
Should you gain fortune and honour,
In this your journey, and task also.'
And he replied: 'God make it so.'

LINES 2979-3020 APPROACH TO THE BRIDGE OF THE SWORD

THE host ceased speaking to his guest,
And once his voice had sunk to rest,
One of the sons followed the knight,
And said: 'We ought to grant outright
All that we have, now, in your service,
Rather than simply yield a promise;
If you have need of us, tis clear
We should not merely linger here,
Waiting for you to ask our aid.

Thus sir, no longer be dismayed
About your horse that sadly died,
We have fine horses here to ride;
I would have you take one of ours,
Choose the best and make it yours,
Take from us aught that you need.'
The knight replied: 'I will indeed.'
Then, their beds having been made,
They retired. And when it was day,
They rose again, early, and dressed,
Ready to leave, both sons and guest.
Upon departure they fail in naught,
But take their leave as they ought
Of master, lady, and all the others.
But I must mention that the brother's
Gift the knight was most unwilling
To accept, and kept insisting,
He would not now mount the steed
Granted to him, though he'd agreed.
Rather he made, as I must recount,
One of the other two it to mount,
The sons who kept him company;
And upon the other's horse did he
Mount, for it pleased him so to do.
When all were astride, the knight too,
All three upon the road did post,
Having taken leave of their host,
Who had, in every way he might,
Served and honoured them the night.
Along the road they went riding,
Until, the evening sun declining,
To the Bridge of the Sword they
Did come, at the ending of the day.

LINES 3021-3194 THE CROSSING

AT the head of this bridge of woe,
They gazed at the water below,
All dismounting from their steeds.
Black and turgid, it raged and seethed,
As foul and dreadful, and as evil
As if twas conjured by the devil.
Then, twas so deep and perilous,
In all the world naught but must
Be lost, in falling, as certainly,
As if it had plunged into the sea.
The bridge that did that gulf breast
Differed, as well, from all the rest;
For never was there such, in sooth.
Never was there, if you seek truth,
So ill a bridge, or so evil a beam;
The bridge across that chill stream,
Was a polished and gleaming blade.
Its steel was strong and well-made,
And at least two lances in length;
And at each end, for greater strength,
A tree-trunk where the blade was set.
And none need fear a fall, as yet,
Due to its bending or shattering,
For such was that blade's tempering
That a massive weight it might bear.
But much discomfort it gave there
To the two in our knight's company;
And they thought that they could see
Over the stream, on the farther side,
A pair of lions, or leopards, tied

To a great rock where the bridge ended.
The stream and the bridge, thus defended,
So filled the two with terror and dread,
Both men trembled with fear and said:
'Take counsel, fair sir, and consider
What it is that you see thither,
For you needs and must so do.
Tis badly made and fashioned too,
This bridge, the carpentry is ill.
If you repent not now at will,
You'll be forced to repent later.
You must indeed now consider
Which course you mean to take,
If you must the crossing make,
Though that thing can never be,
No more than you the wind's free
Flight can halt, so twill not blow,
Or may prevent the birds' song so;
No more than if birds sang a mass,
No more than if it came to pass,
A man re-enter his mother's womb
And be re-born, fresh life assume,
For these are things that cannot be,
No more than emptying the sea;
Do you think that those two fierce
Lions, chained there, will not pierce
You, then kill you, drink the blood
From out your veins, ere they would
Eat your flesh, and gnaw the bones.
Tis enough for me to chance, I own,
To look at them, and meet their eyes;
If you take not good care, say I,
They will devour you, for sure.
Your body they will tear and gnaw,
Inflicting upon you grievous pain.
Mercy they lack, and so will maim.

Have mercy and remain, however,
So that we might stay together!
It would be reprehensible,
To place yourself in mortal peril,
And to do so intentionally.'
The knight replied, then, laughingly:
'Sirs, I must now give thanks to thee,
For showing such concern for me,
It comes of your loveing kindness;
I know you'd ne'er wish distress
On myself, whate'er might chance;
But I with faith and trust advance,
So God will guard me, through all;
I fear nor bridge nor stream, at all,
No more than I fear this dry land;
So ready to cross, here I stand,
And this adventure I shall try,
I'll not turn back, I'd rather die.'
The two sons offer no reply
But from pity they weep and sigh,
Profusely, as well they might;
While, readying himself, the knight
Prepares to cross as best he may;
And does a strange thing this day,
By laying bare his hands and feet;
He shall scarce arrive complete
When he reaches the other side.
Along the sword he now did slide,
Which was sharper than a scythe.
Naked, hands and feet did writhe,
For from his feet he did dispose
Of soles and uppers, then the hose.
And yet the pain he did not dread,
Though bare feet and hands ran red,
Rather he chose to bear it all
Than from the vile bridge to fall

Into that stream, with no egress.
With no small pain and distress,
He crawled across to solid land,
Wounded in feet, knees and hands;
Yet all the suffering and pain
Love, who led him, soothed again,
And, even there, Love made all sweet.
Using his hands and knees and feet,
Thus to the far bank he did slide,
Then looked about from side to side,
Thinking to see those lions there
That the other two had declared
They had seen; he looked around;
But ne'er a lizard there was found,
Or aught else harmful in that place;
He raised his hand towards his face,
And, gazing intently at his ring,
Proved neither lions nor anything
Were present that the two had seen,
For mere enchantment it had been,
And he found nothing living there.
Those on the other side did share
Their joy that he was safe across,
Rightly, and yet more so because
They knew naught of his injuries;
Though he himself was greatly pleased
That he'd not suffered greater harm,
Despite the blood that trickled warm
From his wounds to drench his shirt.
Before him he spied a tower, girt
With stone, right strongly built I mean;
So strong a tower he ne'er had seen.
No finer a tower could one show,
And seated at a high window
Appeared the king, Bademagu,
Most scrupulous, exacting too,

As to honour and what was right,
And it was this king's delight
To prize and practise loyalty.
His son, who, on the contrary,
As far as he might, every day,
Disloyalty loved to display,
And who of working villainy,
And treason, and all felonies,
Never tired, whate'er betide,
Stood there, at the king's side.
They'd seen, from the tower's height,
The painful passage of the knight
Over that bridge of woe and pain.
And Meleagant, the son, was fain
To darken with intense displeasure,
Foreseeing challenge to his seizure
Of the queen; yet he was a knight
Who dreaded no man in a fight,
However fierce or strong he seem,
Nor would there e'er have been
A finer were he not disloyal,
But he had a heart, though royal,
Of stone, devoid of love or pity.
That which made the father happy,
Was sorrow and grief to his son.
The king, indeed, knew the one
Who had crossed the bridge to be
Far greater a knight than any;
For no man would have spent
Such pains in whom ill-intent
Dwelt, that shames the evil more
Than virtue the good doth honour;
And virtue's works seem ever less
Than those of idle wickedness,
For, beyond doubt, tis ever true,
More evil than good may we do.

Lines 3195-3318 King Bademagu and his son Meleagant disagree

MORE on this subject I could say,
If so to do caused not delay;
But to other matters I must turn,
Who to my tale shall now return.
And you shall hear how the king
Schools his son in this very thing:
'My son,' says he, 'it proved good,
That we, here, at the window stood
Both you and I, and thus perceived
As reward, what must surely be
The greatest deed that e'er was wrought,
Or of which any man e'er thought,
Performed by a knight, as we saw.
Tell me now if you are not more
Well-disposed towards the man
Who fulfilled this wondrous plan.
Make peace, and release the queen!
Scant glory shall you gain, I ween,
But rather great harm shall arise,
If you fight. Show yourself wise,
And courteous, and send the queen
To him ere you yourself are seen.
Show him honour in our country,
And that which he has come to seek
Grant to him ere he makes demand;
For you know well and understand
He comes seeking Queen Guinevere.
Do not be seen as stubborn here,
Or viewed as one foolish and proud!

If, all alone, he comes here now,
Then you should keep him company,
For noble with noble should agree,
And each show the other honour,
Not be strangers to one another.
Honour to him who honour shows;
Honour will thus be yours, I know,
If you show honour and do service
To one who showed himself by this,
The best knight in the world today.'
'God confound me,' his son did say,
'If as good or better is not found here!'
Ill done, that he did not hide, I fear,
That he thought himself no less a man.
He added: 'Kneeling, with clasped hands,
You'd see me swear myself as his,
And hold my lands in his service?
God help me, I'd rather be seen
As his than surrender the queen!
God forbid that in such a manner
I should agree to her surrender!
She'll never be rendered up by me,
But rather defended, endlessly,
Against all who foolishly dare,
In search of her, to hither fare.'
Then said the king to him again:
'My son, were you but to refrain
From this twould be more courteous.
I pray you maintain peace among us.
You know that honour will belong
To this knight if he waxes strong
And wins her from you in battle.'
He'd rather win her so I can tell
Than through all your courtesy,
For that would increase his glory.

It seems to me he seeks her here
Not that he might to peace adhere,
But rather to regain her by force.
So twould be your wisest course,
Not to fight with him recklessly.
That you are foolish saddens me,
And, if my counsel you despise,
Twill prove worse for you than I,
And evil will come to you, I fear,
For this knight in his sojourn here
Has none to trouble him but you.
As for myself, and household too,
I'll offer him peace and security,
I've ne'er acted with disloyalty,
Committed treason or felony,
Nor will for you do villainy,
Any more than for a stranger;
Nor will prefer you, but rather
I hereby promise that the knight
Shall lack for naught that he might
Need; armour, steed shall be his own,
Due to the courage he has shown
In coming to our kingdom thus.
And he shall be defended by us,
Against all other men here too,
And protected, except from you.
And I would have him understand
That, if against you he shall stand,
He need have fear of none other.'
'I have listened, in silence, father,
Long enough,' said Meleagant,
'You may say whate'er you want,
But little I care for all your speech.
Tis no hermit, to whom you preach,
Filled with pity, and charitable,

Nor shall I be so honourable
As to give him what I most prize.
His object he'll not realise
So easily, nor half so soon,
As you and he may both conceive.
We need not quarrel, I believe,
Even if you should aid him so.
If with you and your household
He makes peace, what's that to me?
Naught in my heart fails, for, see,
I'm the more pleased, God save me,
That he need fear myself merely.
I wish you to do for me naught,
Not a thing that might be thought
To smack of disloyalty or treason.
Play as you please the virtuous one,
And leave it to me to be cruel.'
'What? You will not yield, you mule?'
'No,' said he. 'Then words shall cease.
 Do your best; I leave you in peace,
And I'll go speak to this knight.
For I'll now offer him outright
My aid and my counsel in all;
I'll take his side, whate'er befall.

LINES 3319-3490 KING BADEMAGU OFFERS THE KNIGHT OF THE CART HIS AID

THE king descended to the court,
And had his royal charger brought.
To him was led a handsome steed,
And he mounted promptly indeed,
Taking some few for company,

A pair of squires, and knights three,
Who go with him, and none beside.
Nor did they cease from their ride
Till of the bridgehead they had sight.
Arriving there, they found the knight
Wiping his wounds free of blood;
This man, the king now understood,
Must be his guest till all was well,
Though the king felt, truth to tell,
That one might sooner drain the sea.
Then the king dismounted swiftly,
And the sorely wounded knight
At once dragged himself upright,
Though twas the king he knew not,
As if all his anguish were forgot,
All the pain in his hands and feet,
And he himself sound and complete.
The king, at the effort this incurred,
Hurried to greet him, with kind word:
'Sir, I am occupied with wonder
At how you've come from yonder,
To fall upon us in this country.
Be welcome, for it seems to me,
None will attempt the like again.
That past and future, as is plain,
Saw not, nor shall see, such a deed,
Or meet such peril, I must concede.
And know that I love you the more
For doing what no man has before
Either himself conceived, or dared.
You will find me disposed to care
For you; and true and courteous.
And I, as the king here, among us,
Offer you, willingly, all there is
Of my good counsel and service;

And know, full well, my thinking
As to what you come here seeking,
For I believe you seek the queen.'
'Yes, sire,' he said, 'and her I mean
To find; naught else brings me here.'
'Friend, you'll suffer pain, I fear,'
Said the king, 'ere you regain her.
And I see you already suffer;
I see your wounds, and the blood.
He'll not be generous, as I would,
He who led her here, that knight,
And surrender her without a fight.
But you must stay, so we may see
To your wounds, till you may be
Healed, and are whole completely.
The ointment of the Three Mary's,
Or a better if such may be found,
I will give, that you may be sound,
Seeking thus your health and ease.
The queen is so imprisoned she's
Not accessible to mortal man,
Not even my son, Meleagant,
Who led her here, and takes it ill.
Ne'er did man with rage so fill
As he, who's sore and angry too.
But I, who look kindly upon you,
So help me God, will gladly give
Whate'er you need, as I do live.
Not even my son, who I will not
Favour in this, armour has got
As fine as that I shall give you
And the horse that you need too.
Whoever is angered, yet I will
Protect you from all others still.
And you need fear no man, I say,

Except the one who brought away
Queen Guinevere and led her here.
None's been so berated, I fear,
As this son of mine has by me,
Well nigh driven from this country
By my displeasure, for that he
Will not surrender her to thee.
He is my son, but trouble not,
For he shall never do you a jot
Of harm, against my will, unless
In battle with you he prove best.'
'I give you thanks, sire!' he replied,
'Yet time is a-wasting here, say I,
Time indeed that I would not waste.
Naught of this is to my distaste,
Nor do my wounds hinder me.
Lead me then to wherever we
May meet, for with this my armour
I will happily endeavour
To render blows and blows receive.'
'Friend, twould be better to leave
Such matters for a fortnight or so,
To see your wounds healed or no.
Best if you stay with me, sir knight,
And for at least this next fortnight.
For I'll not suffer it, anyway,
Nor could I witness the display,
If you were to fight before me
With the arms and gear I see.'
And he replied, 'If it so please,
No other weapons than these
Would I willingly use to fight
This battle, nor do seek respite,
Nor adjournment, nor delay,
But would fight with these today.

Yet, in deference to you, I state
That till tomorrow I will wait,
But then whate'er any may say
I shall brook no further delay.'
And so the king replied, to this,
He should have his every wish,
And had him to his lodgings led,
And then to all his servants said
They must serve him well that day,
And they did willingly obey.
Then the king who gladly would
Have wrought a truce if he could,
Went straight away to see his son,
And, speaking to him then as one
Who wished for peace and accord,
Said: 'Fair son, cease this discord,
Be reconciled without a fight!'
He has not come here, this knight,
To chase the deer or hunt the boar,
He comes here in search of honour,
To enhance his praise and renown,
And he is much in need, I found,
Of rest and healing; would that he
Had taken good counsel from me,
So I this battle need not expect,
Neither this month or the next,
Of which he seems so desirous.
What could prove so disastrous
About your rendering him the queen?
Fear no dishonour, that I mean,
For on you will fall no blame.
Rather tis wrong now to retain
That to which you have no right.
Most willingly would this knight
Engage in battle straight away,

Though his hands and feet, I say,
Are not whole, but cut and raw.'
'Right foolish you are, and more,'
Said Meleagant, to his father,
'By the faith I owe Saint Peter,
I'll hear you not in this affair.
If I did so, torn apart, I swear,
By horses, I'd deserve to die.
If he seeks honour, so do I.
If he seeks glory, I seek mine.
And if he wishes battle, fine,
That I wish a hundred times more.'
'Set on blind folly, as before,
Folly you'll find,' said the king,
'Tomorrow you may try the thing,
Since you so please, with this knight.'
'May no more troublesome a fight'
Said Meleagant, 'visit me ever!
I wish it were this day rather
Than that it should be tomorrow.
See my countenance of sorrow;
I look more downcast than before.
My eyes are wilder than of yore,
And much paler seems my face.
Until I meet him, tis the case
That I'll have neither joy nor ease,
Nor is there aught that can please.'

LINES 3491-3684 THE KNIGHT IS REVEALED AS LANCELOT OF THE LAKE

THE king could see by his manner
Advice was useless, as was prayer,

And dismissed his son, reluctantly,
Chose arms and a good strong steed,
And sent them for him to enjoy
Who was worthy of their employ.
There he also sent a surgeon,
One known as a good Christian,
And none more trusted anywhere,
A doctor more skilled in such care,
Than all those of Montpellier;
And he treated the knight that day,
With all the means that were to hand,
In accord with the king's command.
The news had gone abroad already
Among all the lords and ladies,
And the maidens and the knights,
And set the country round alight;
And all that night, until broad day,
Friends and strangers made their way
Toward the castle, hour by hour.
By morning, all about the tower,
So great a crowd had gathered, there
Was not a foot of ground to spare.
And in the morn the king arose,
The battle adding to his sorrows,
And went first thing to see his son,
Who'd but now laced his helmet on,
A helm well-made in Poitiers;
Since there could now be no delay,
Nor was there any chance of peace,
For though his efforts did not cease,
The king's attempts lacked power.
Amid the square, before the tower,
According to the king's command,
Where all the people now did stand,
Was the place where they would fight.

The king sent for the unknown knight,
At once, and led him to the square.
Which was tight-packed everywhere,
With folk from the realm of Logres.
For as they to the church progress
Each year, to hear the organ play,
On Pentecost, or Christmas Day,
As they're accustomed so to do,
So all the folk had gathered too
Here, in assembly, in full array.
And for the space of three days,
All the foreign maidens there
From Arthur's court, feet bared,
In their shifts, had fasted straight,
So that God might of his great
Grace grant strength and virtue
In the fight that must now ensue
To him who for the captives fought.
While those of Bademagu's court
Prayed on behalf of the young lord
God would him the honours afford,
And grant to him the victory.
Ere prime did sound, full early,
Both of the knights, now were led
To the square, armed from foot to head,
On horses clad with plates of steel.
Meleagant came to the field
Handsome, graceful and alert,
With his close-knit mail shirt,
And his helmet, and his shield
That his neck and side concealed;
All these did become him well.
But as to the other, all could tell,
Even those who wished him ill,
And vowed, that Meleagant was still

Worth naught compared to this knight.
As soon as they were placed aright,
In the square, the king appeared,
Detained them, as the time neared,
Seeking peace, before everyone,
But yet could not persuade his son;
And so he said: 'Now grasp the rein,
And you your eager steeds restrain,
Until I've mounted to the tower.
This small favour's in your power,
To wait a moment more for me.'
Then he left them, sorrowfully,
And to that very place did climb,
Where he knew that he would find
The queen, who the night before
Had asked that he might afford
To her a clear view of the fight.
This he had granted her outright,
So now he went to escort her,
Concerned to show her honour,
And serve her with all courtesy.
At one window there sat she,
And at another, upon her right,
He sat to view the coming fight.
And also sitting with those two
There was many a knight too,
And prudent lady, and a band
Of maidens born in that land;
And there were many prisoners
All intent upon their prayers,
Who were captive in that country.
For our knight they prayed, freely,
And their orisons did sayeth.
In God and him they place their faith
And hopes of deliverance.

Then both the knights advance,
Forcing the folk to move aside,
Clash shields with elbows as they ride,
Gripping them with their arms fiercely,
Each strikes the other so violently
Through the shield he drives his lance;
Two arms' length deep it doth advance.
Cracks like a branch in the fire's heat;
While head to head the horses meet,
And clash together breast to breast;
And shield on shield, in this contest,
And helmet doth with helmet clash,
Much as doth peal the thunder crash,
Which echoes with so great a sound
It seems to shake the solid ground.
Never a breast-strap, girth or rein,
But parted sharply with the strain,
Nor surcingle; their saddle-bows,
Though strong, were broken by the blows.
Twas no great shame that these two
Both tumbled to the ground, in view
Of their sudden misadventure.
They leap to their feet, to ensure
Both can fight on once more,
Fiercer than boar against boar;
And do all threatening words forego,
To deal, with the blade, blow on blow,
Like men whom hatred doth renew.
Often they slice so fiercely through
Helmet, or gleaming coat of mail,
The blood springs forth without fail.
A fine battle they did provide,
Inflicting wounds on either side,
From heavy blows that on them rained.
Many fierce bouts they long sustained,

Struggling together mutually,
Such that the onlookers could see
No advantage to either knight.
But it was plain that in the fight
He who had crossed the bridge must be
Much hampered by his hands which he
Had wounded, in entering that land.
Much dismayed were those on hand,
Full many inclined to his side,
Seeing his blows falling wide,
Thinking he would defeated be.
Now weakening, it seemed that he
Would have the worst of the fight while
Meleagant would win in style;
And all around began to murmur.
But at the window of the tower
Sat a maid who was full wise,
And of herself she did surmise
The knight did not thus undertake
The dread encounter for her sake,
Or for these folk that stood about,
Who merely came to watch the bout,
But that his only thought had been
Simply to battle for the queen;
And she thought that if he knew
The queen sat at the window too,
So that she might the battle view,
His strength and courage would renew.
And if she had but known his name,
She would have cried out the same,
That he might look above his head;
So she came to the queen and said:
'Lady, for God's and for your sake
And ours, this enquiry I make,
As to the name of that brave knight,

So I may aid him in the fight.
Tell me his name, if you do know.'
'The question that you ask doth show,
Fair maiden,' replied the queen,
'No hatred or ill, but it has been
Asked with good intent, I see.
His name I know, for he must be
Lancelot of the Lake, this knight.'
'God! How my heart fills with delight,'
Exclaimed the maid, and cried aloud,
Leaning forward, above the crowd,
Such that, whether they would or not,
All heard her calling: 'Lancelot!
Turn about now that you may see,
Who it is who takes note of thee.'

LINES 3685-3954 KING BADEMAGU BRINGS ABOUT
CONDITIONAL PEACE

WHEN Lancelot heard the shout,
He was not slow to turn about;
He turned, and there, high above,
The thing which he most did love,
Of all that in the world might be,
At the tower window, he did see.
From the moment that he saw her
He turned not again, nor from her
Moved the direction of his gaze;
Meleagant, in all the ways
He could, forcing the attack,
While Lancelot guarded his back.
Meleagant was filled with joy
Seeing the tactics so deployed;

His folk too were all delighted,
While the foreigners, affrighted,
Could scarce hold themselves upright,
Falling to their knees in fright,
Or lying prone upon the ground;
On one side, glad cries did sound,
But, on the other, shouts of pain.
Then the maiden called again,
From the window, up on high:
'Ah! Lancelot! Now tell me why
You must behave so foolishly?
You were the height of chivalry,
Indeed, a paragon of virtue;
I never thought it could be true
That God would ever make a knight
Who could match you in a fight,
Or equal your worth and valour.
Now we see you well-nigh waver,
Lashing out with backhand blows,
Behind you, fending off your foe.
Move, so you're on the other side,
Keep the tower before your eyes,
Such that you'll not be blamed.'
Then Lancelot felt sore ashamed,
And angry with himself that he,
Had for a while, as all could see,
Suffered the worst of the fight,
Nor fought as fiercely as he might.
So he leapt back and, by force,
Placed Meleagant on a course
Between himself and the tower,
While Meleagant used his power
In trying to regain his place.
But Lancelot runs in apace,
And strikes him so violently,

Upon his body and his shield,
Whene'er he seeks to win ground,
That he is forced to whirl around,
Once or twice, at every blow.
Lancelot's strength and courage grow,
Partly because Love grants him aid,
Partly because he's ne'er displayed
Such hatred as towards this man;
With none has he been so enraged
As him with whom he is engaged.
Such love and such mortal hate,
That ne'er before waxed so great,
Made him so valorous and bold,
That Meleagant began to hold
Him in awe, the fight no jest;
For ne'er had he in fierce contest
Known or met with such a knight,
Nor been so wounded in the fight
By any knight, as now by this.
Further danger he would miss,
So must he sidestep and evade,
Hating the blows and half-afraid.
Nor were Lancelot's threats in vain;
He pushed him to the tower again,
Where the queen watched on high.
Doing homage, he came so nigh
The tower's wall that he was now
So very close to it, I vow,
That he must cease to see her face
Should he advance another pace.
Thus Lancelot oft drove him so
Hither and thither, to and fro,
In whatever manner he pleased,
And always halting, when he ceased,
Before the queen, his lady fair,

She who had kindled the flame there
Which did make him gaze so on her.
While the flame, in his heart, doth stir
Him so against Meleagant,
He can press him as he wants,
Driving him from place to place!
He leads him to and fro, apace,
Whether he will or no, resigned,
Like a cripple, or one who's blind.
The king, seeing his son hard-pressed,
Is troubled, and pities his distress,
And would aid him speedily;
Yet to do so courteously
He must ask it of the queen.
So he began: 'Since you have been
In my keep, Lady, and my purlieu,
I've loved, and served, and honoured you,
And naught that could be said and done
Has been willingly left undone
Which might be added to your honour;
Now reward me with your favour.
A boon I'd have you now approve
You should not grant except for love.
My son, pitted against my guest,
Now has the worst of this contest,
Yet not for that reason do I speak,
But that this Lancelot may not seek
His death, having him in his power;
Nor ought you, in such an hour;
For though he has not done well
By you, and wronged him as well,
Yet for me, who do beg you now,
Of your mercy, this boon allow,
That he not seek to kill my son.
For, if you do, then that guerdon

Repays all I have done for you.'
'Fair sire, I am willing so to do,
At your request,' replied the queen.
'For even if my hatred had been
Mortal, toward your son, whom I
Do not love, yet so well in my
Service have you acted, to please
You I'd wish Lancelot to cease.'
And these were not merely words
Spoken in private, but were heard
By Lancelot and Meleagant.
Lovers are ever compliant,
And, where perfect love exists,
Swiftly, and willingly, insist
On what gives their mistress' pleasure.
So must Lancelot, in full measure,
Who loved more than Pyramus,
If any man could e'er love thus.
Lancelot heard all her speech;
As soon as the last word reached
His ears from her lips, he cried:
'Such a request I'll not deny,
Since you wish it, and will halt.'
Now Lancelot dared not assault
His foe, or make the slightest move,
Even though his foe might prove
Hostile, and thus seek his death.
He moved not, scarce drew a breath,
While the other still tried to maim
Him, feeling both wrath and shame,
That they'd been forced to intervene.
For now the king had left the queen
And had descended, to upbraid him,
And entering the list delayed him,
Speaking sharply at their meeting:

'How now, my son, is this fitting,
That he moves not, yet you strike?
You are too harsh and too warlike;
Your prowess is misplaced indeed,
For without doubt all are agreed,
He's shown he's your superior.'
Then Meleagant, in anger,
Choking with shame, replies:
'You've lost the use of your eyes!
I doubt that you could see a thing,
He is blind who dies believing
That I was not the better man.'
'Find any who think other than
That very thing!' the king replies,
'For all the folk here know who lies,
And whether you speak truth or no.'
Then to his barons the king doth go,
And bids them lead his son away
And they in turn make no delay
In carrying out the king's command,
Departing with Meleagant;
But to draw Lancelot away
Scant force was required that day,
For he would have suffered woe,
Before he'd have touched his foe.
Then the king addressed his son:
'So help me God, at last, have done,
Make peace, and render up the queen.
This whole quarrel that lies between
You and he must cease today.'
'What nonsense, you ever say!
A wealth of nothing you declare!
Away! Leave us to our affair,
And do not tangle with our fight!'
Said the king: 'Such is not right;

127

Since that this knight would kill you now
If I did leave you, all allow.'
'Kill me? Tis most certain that I
Will kill the man rather than die,
If you'd but let us fight again;
We would see who conquered then.'
The king replied: 'Now, yet again,
So help me God, you speak in vain.'
'Why?' 'Since I wish it not,' said he,
'Neither in your pride nor folly
Will I so trust, and see you die.
Mad is he who seeks death, say I,
As you do now, unwise I trow.
That you hate me, well I know,
Because I seek to protect you.
God will not let me thus view
Your death, when I wish otherwise;
Too great the grief that would arise.'
His son he reproved, till concord
And peace was once again restored;
The terms of the truce such that he
To surrender the queen must agree,
If Lancelot consented to be
Summoned, and would willingly,
And within a year from the day
Of the summons, its terms obey:
To fight with Meleagant again.
This pact yields Lancelot no pain.
Peace being nigh, folk gather round,
And they suggest the battleground
Should be at King Arthur's court;
There twas right it should be fought,
He holding Britain, and Cornwall.
The queen must now consent to all,
And Lancelot yield up his promise,

That if Meleagant conquer in this,
She and he must return together,
And none there seek to detain her.
The queen with all this concurred,
And then Lancelot gave his word,
And thus both sides were in accord,
And so resigned lance and sword.
The custom was in that country
That if one prisoner were set free,
All others might quit their prisons;
On Lancelot they rained benisons.
And you might rightfully surmise
That joy now shone in his two eyes,
And so it did, with nary a doubt.
The prisoners stood round about,
And they in Lancelot rejoiced,
Speaking aloud, as with one voice:
'Sire, to us, in all truth, joy came,
As soon as we had heard your name,
For then we knew with certainty,
That we would thus delivered be.'
A great crowd about him pressed,
Pushing and striving to express
Their joy, and touch him if they could.
And those who succeeded in this
Were overjoyed, such was their bliss.
There was joy there but sorrow too,
For though all those freed from prison
Expressed their joy with abandon,
Meleagant and his countrymen
Saw nothing that delighted them;
All dark and pensive, sad of face.
The king now turned from that place,
Nor was Lancelot left behind,
Who begged him he might find

His way, that instant, to the queen.
'I shall not fail; she shall be seen,'
Said the king, 'for it seems right,
And if you wish me to, sir knight,
I'll show you Kay, the Seneschal.'
Such joy had Lancelot withal,
He well-nigh knelt at the king's feet;
But they now passed on to meet
The queen, where she sat in state,
In the hall, and did both await.

LINES 3955-4030 QUEEN GUINEVERE IS DISPLEASED

ON seeing the king, who by the hand
Led Lancelot, the queen did stand,
Then curtsied low before the king;
Yet seeming angered at something,
With clouded brow, no word said she.
'You see here, Lancelot, lady'
Said the king, 'who comes to view
His queen; that should bring joy to you.'
'I, sire? Me he cannot please,
To see his face gives me no ease.'
'Come now, Lady,' said the king
Courteous, frank, in everything,
'Why do you adopt this stance?
You are too scornful of a man
Who has served you and loyally,
Such that he has oft on his journey
Exposed himself to mortal danger,
And rescued and defends you ever
Against Meleagant, my son,
Who to you great wrong has done.'

'Sire, in truth, tis an ill employ;
For my part, I feel no annoy
In saying that I thank him not.'
Now this astonished Lancelot,
Yet he responded, however,
In the manner of a true lover:
'Lady, though that surely grieves me,
I'll not ask a reason of thee.'
Thus Lancelot voiced his sorrow,
While the queen his speech did follow,
But so to grieve him and confound
Him, not one word did she sound,
But hence, to her room, did depart.
Lancelot sent both eyes and heart
To the doorway, following after,
But, the nearness of her chamber
Meant his eyes must swiftly lose her;
He would gladly have pursued her,
Had that been possible, I'm sure,
But the heart, which is the more
Lord and master, and doth possess
Much greater power, now did press
On behind her, leaving, sadly,
Eyes full of tears, with the body.
In private now the king addressed
Lancelot; wonder he expressed:
'What can this mean, how can it be
That the queen should refuse to see,
And is unwilling to speak to, you?
If she was accustomed so to do,
She should not disdain you now,
Nor speech with yourself disallow,
After all you have done for her.
So tell me then, if you know, sir,
Why for you she's shown, indeed

Such bitter scorn, for what misdeed?'
'I took no note, sire' said Lancelot,
'Yet the sight of me pleases her not,
Nor will she listen to aught I say,
It troubles and grieves me alway.'
'Surely,' the king said, 'she does wrong,'
For you well-nigh risked death not long
Ago for her, amidst certain danger.
Fair sweet friend, let us not linger,
We'll go speak with the Seneschal.'
He replied: 'I'll gladly go withal.'
So to the Seneschal they went.
Straight upon Lancelot's advent;
The very first word that Sir Kay,
The Seneschal, to him did say,
Was: 'How you do shame me!' 'How so?'
Said Lancelot, 'that I may know,
Tell me what shame I've brought on you.'
'That you have done what I couldn't do,
Brings shame on me, as I believe;
For twas a thing I could not achieve.'

LINES 4031-4124 LANCELOT SETS OUT FOR THE SUNKEN BRIDGE

THEN the king left them together,
And issued alone from the chamber,
And Lancelot asked the Seneschal
If there he'd met with ill at all.
'Yes, and still do so, I avow,
I ne'er met with such ill as now,'
He said, 'and I were dead long ago,
If not for the king, who doth show,

Out of his compassion and pity,
For me such kindness and amity,
That he would not knowingly
Let me lack for aught I might need;
For there is not a single thing
That to me they fail to bring,
As soon as he of it doth hear.
But against his goodness, I fear,
Meleagant takes the other part,
His son, all filled with evil art,
Who hath doctors, that here, on hand,
And treacherously, at his command,
Ointments to my wounds apply,
That must destroy me, by and by.
Thus have I father and step-father,
For when the king applies a plaster
To my wounds to do me good,
Wishing to ease me as it should,
So I might be healed completely,
Comes the son and treacherously
Seeking to kill me, then removes
All swiftly, and a traitor proves,
Replacing it with vile ointment.
But that tis not the king's intent,
I am as certain as I can be:
Such a murderous felony
He'd not in any way condone.
And of the courtesy he's shown
To my lady, you know naught.
Never did man so guard a fort
As vigilantly, I must remark,
Since old Noah built his Ark,
As he has guarded this lady;
For he forbade his son to see
The queen, though much aggrieved,

Except in courtly company,
Or in his own royal presence.
The honour shown her is immense,
And up to this present moment,
The king, of his mercy, is content,
To grant her all she might devise.
None could devise more, I surmise,
For she devises all that is done.
And the king prizes her, for one,
For the trust in him she has shown.
But is it true, as seems well known,
That she is so angry towards you
That, before all, she has refused
To speak with you, ne'er a word?'
'The truth, indeed, you have heard,'
Said Lancelot, 'the thing is so.
But tell me now, if you know,
For God's sake, why she is displeased.'
Kay replied he could not conceive
The reason, twas wondrous strange.
'Well let it be as she doth arrange,'
Said Lancelot, twas all he could say,
'For I must now be upon my way,
And I'll go seek my Lord Gawain,
Who with me entered on this terrain,
And who agreed that he would go
To the Sunken Bridge; thus I follow.'
He left the room, and swiftly went
To inform the king of his intent,
And asked his leave to go his way.
The king said willingly that he may.
But those that Lancelot had freed
From captivity, by his brave deed,
Asked him what they were to do.
And he replied: 'All those of you

Who wish may come along with me.
While those of you who'd rather be
At the queen's side may remain;
Such is your right, I do maintain.'
Those who wished all went with him,
More joyous now than they had been,
While with the queen there remained
Her maids, whom pleasure detained,
And many a knight and lady too;
And yet not one remained, tis true,
Who would not rather have gone
To their own country than stay on.
But thus the queen kept them near,
Waiting for Lord Gawain to appear,
Saying she'd make no move to leave
Till news of him she did receive.

LINES 4125-4262 GUINEVERE GRIEVES ON FALSE NEWS OF LANCELOT'S DEATH

EVERYWHERE the news doth spread
That the queen from prison is led,
And the captives are now set free,
And may go about at liberty,
As it suits, when and wherever.
All the natives gather together,
Seeking the truth, as to what befell,
And cannot talk about aught else.
And all are angered that, at last,
The perilous ways have been passed,
So all, may come and go, as they please:
And naught is as it was wont to be!
And when the folk of that country

135

Who knew not, heard of the victory
That Lancelot achieved in the fight,
They took themselves to where they might
Have sight of him as he passed along
Thinking that they could do no wrong
In the king's eyes, surely, if they
Seized Lancelot, and drew him away.
His men were all unarmed and thus,
When the natives, who waxed furious,
Came at them all armed, no wonder
That Lancelot must there surrender,
Our knight being unarmed also.
A prisoner back now he must go,
His feet tied beneath his horse,
While his men said: 'You, by force,
Do evil, sirs, for the king's decree
Protects us; in his safe care go we.'
But they said: 'Of that we know naught,
But as we have seized you, to the court
You must go, and immediately.'
Then news was brought, erroneously,
To the king that his folk had seized him,
Then bound Lancelot, and killed him.
Great was his sorrow when he heard,
By his head he swore, and his word
Went out, that the killers would die.
No quarter must to them apply,
And, if they could but be found,
They must be hanged, or burned, or drowned.
If with rope, or fire, or water nigh,
They should attempt to deny
The deed, he'd not believe a word,
For, upon his heart, that vile herd
Had brought such sorrow and shame
Disgrace would e'er tarnish his name

If he did not his vengeance take;
Vengeance he'd have and no mistake!
The tidings spread, and flew unseen,
Until their import reached the queen,
Seated there, dining, at her table.
She almost died, hearing the fable,
The false news that had been brought,
Of the death of brave Lancelot;
For she believed what they did say,
And was plunged in such deep dismay
She well-nigh lost the power to speak;
Yet for those around her said, openly:
'Truly, his death it grieves me much,
And tis not wrong it should do such,
For he did come to this land for me,
And on that account I should grieve.'
Then she murmurs to herself low,
That none can hear her murmur so,
Saying that no one there need pray
Her to eat or drink, that or any day,
If true word of his death they give,
He for whom she alone doth live.
Then she rises, on sorrow intent,
And, to herself, she doth lament,
So that none hears her or takes note.
Now she grasps often at her throat,
As if she is bent on her own death,
And confesses, beneath her breath,
Her own sin, one towards himself;
Blaming, and reproaching, herself,
For the wrong that she has wrought,
Against one whom she has thought
To be her own, and been hers ever,
And had he lived, proved so forever.
So distressed is she by her cruelty,

That it greatly mars her beauty,
For her cruelty and her disdain
Now do prove her beauty's bane
More than all her vigils together
And her fasting marred it ever.
All her misdeeds, as one, arise;
She reviews them and often cries:
'Alas! What was I thinking of
When before me stood my love,
That I disdained to greet him there,
And would not hear his words so fair?
When I denied him speech and look,
Was that not pure folly, to brook?
Folly? Rather, so God help me,
All was violence and cruelty.
As a jest I intended it, but no,
No jest; he did not think it so
For indeed he pardoned me not.
None but myself killed Lancelot;
The mortal blow was mine alone.
When all smiling he was shown
To where I was, thinking that I
Would welcome him, by and by,
And not a glance did I bestow;
Was not that then a mortal blow?
When my speech I did him deny,
At once, with that blow then, did I
Rob him of heart and life together.
Those twin blows his life did sever.
No other murderer caused his death.
Dear God! Can I ever, by my faith,
Atone for this murder, for this crime?
Never, indeed, sooner shall time
Drain all the rivers and the seas!
Alas! What comfort it would be,

How it would heal me, if that I
For just one moment, ere he died
Had held him here in my two arms.
What? Naked, laid bare my charms,
The better my joy in him to take.
If he's dead, twould prove my mistake
Were I not to take my life also.
How can it hurt my lover though
If after his death I am still living,
If I take no pleasure in anything
Except this sorrow I harbour so?
If after his death such grief I know,
Sweet to him, could he see it, this,
This deep sorrow that now I wish.
Wrong is she who would rather die
Than weep for her lover, and sigh.
Surely it is sweeter that I,
In lengthy mourning, grieve and cry.
I'd rather live, and suffer blows,
Than die and in the grave repose.'

Lines 4263-4414 Lancelot grieves on false news of Guinevere's death

FOR two days the queen mourned so,
And to all food and drink said no,
Until all thought that she must die.
Many are those who will, say I,
Carry bad news rather than good.
The tidings Lancelot understood
Were of his love's and lady's death.
Great was then his sorrow, i'faith;
It was clear to all folk that he

139

Was sad and most melancholy.
Indeed, if you would know the truth
He was so downcast, forsooth,
He held his life as little worth,
Wishing soon to leave this earth;
But first arose his long lament.
A running noose, with sad intent,
He knotted at one end of his belt,
Weeping, sighing the pain he felt:
'Ah! Death! How you do ensnare me,
And, in my prime, now destroy me!
I am brought low, yet feel no ill,
Except this grief that doth me kill.
This grief is ill, in truth tis mortal.
Yet I would wish it so, withal,
And, if God wills it, I shall die.
Yet is there no other way that I
Can die, without God's consent?
Yes, if He sanctions my intent,
To place this noose about my neck,
For I may then my own death effect
And, even against Death's will, die so.
For Death indeed only covets those
Who fear to die, and will come not,
To me, yet with this selfsame knot
I'll draw Death near, this very hour,
And once I have Death in my power,
Then Death shall execute my wish.
Truly, Death proves too slow in this,
Such my longing to grasp Death now!'
Then no more time doth he allow,
But over his head slips the noose,
Then about his neck, still loose,
And then so its full effect be felt,
Fastens now the end of the belt

Tightly about his saddle-bow,
Such that his men do not know.
Then he lets himself slip down,
So that thus, to his charger bound,
He might be dragged to his death,
Disdaining another hour of breath.
But when the rest of his company
Witness him falling, perilously,
They suppose him to be in a faint,
For none can see the tight constraint
Of the noose looped round his neck.
Swift, in their embrace, they collect
Their lord, supporting him together,
Thus do they all the noose discover,
Which about his throat he'd placed,
Thinking he had Death embraced.
Swiftly the belt they did sever;
The tightness of the noose however
Had done his throat so much harm
That for a while his voice was gone;
The veins in all his neck and throat
Swollen so much he'd almost choked;
Yet now, even if twas his will,
He could do himself no more ill.
It grieved him they had wrought so;
He was consumed with rage also
For he would willingly have died
If they his action had not espied.
Now that he could catch his breath,
He cried: 'Ah, vile shameless Death,
By God, why had you not the power,
And virtue to slay me ere that hour
When my lady was doomed to die?
Twas because you would not, say I,
Deign to have done so kind a deed,

Spared me, through villainy indeed,
And of you one may expect no less.
Ah! What service and what kindness!
How well you now employ them here!
Cursed be the man who gives you fair
Thanks for such service as this I see!
I know not who's more my enemy,
Life that makes me weep and sigh,
Or Death that will not let me die,
One or the other torments me so;
Yet, God help me, tis right I know,
That despite myself, I live on.
I should have been dead and gone,
Once indeed my lady the queen
Showed such hatred of me, I mean.
She'd not do so from ill intention,
Rather she did so with good reason,
Although I know not what that was.
But if I'd known what was the cause,
Before her spirit to God ascended,
Then my fault had been amended,
So as to please her, and so richly
She'd have granted me her mercy.
Lord! What could my crime have been?
I think she knew that I was seen
To have clambered onto the cart.
What other crime twas I know not
If not that. That has undone me.
If twas for that she did hate me,
Lord! Why should that deed harm me?
For any who sought to reproach me,
Must indeed know naught of Love;
No mouth should open to reprove
A single thing that for Love is done,
Love that rules lovers, every one.

Tis a mark of love and courtesy,
Whatever one does for one's lady.
And yet for 'my love' I did it not.
Ah, what to call her I know not!
Whether to say 'my love' or no,
I dare not call her such, I know.
But of love this I know, I'd deem,
She should have shown no less esteem
For me, if she loved me ever,
But rather called me her true lover,
When an honour it seemed to me
To do whatever Love asked of me,
Even to clamber onto the cart.
She should have charged it to the heart;
For there was proof if e'er there be,
That Love thus tries the devotee,
And so identifies Love's own.
Yet her displeasure was shown,
At such service; as I discovered,
By the face she showed her lover.
And yet for her he did that deed
For which many others decreed
That he bear reproach and shame.
And for that act me they do blame,
And turn to bitterness my sweet,
I'faith, for such treatment they mete
Out to us, knowing naught of love,
And honour itself shameful prove:
And he who dips honour in shame,
Cleanses it not but soils the same;
They are but ignorant of Love,
Who go thus despising Love,
Who far above Love would appear,
And Love's commands do not fear.
For, without fail, the better man

Is he who honours Love's command.
All things are pardonable there;
He's the coward who does not dare.'

LINES 4415-4440 LANCELOT AND GUINEVERE HEAR THAT THE OTHER STILL LIVES

THUS Lancelot doth make lament,
And they all grieve who are intent
On his care, his protection too.
And news arrives as they so do,
That the queen is, in truth, not dead.
Then Lancelot is comforted,
And if he had felt grief before,
Thinking her dead, his joy is more,
A thousand times greater again,
Is this delight than was the pain.
They found themselves that day,
But six or seven leagues away
From King Bademagu's seat,
And thus the king had receipt
Of pleasing news of Lancelot:
That he had reached that very spot,
And was alive, both safe and sound.
The king, all courtesy, went and found
The queen, and gave the news to her.
And she replied to him: 'Fair sir,
Since you say it, I know tis true.
An if he were dead, I swear to you
That I would ne'er feel joy again.
For all my joy would turn to pain,
If, in my service, a true knight
Was slain, and he denied a fight.'

LINES 4441-4530 THE LOVERS ARE RECONCILED

THEN from her the king did part,
While the queen longed in her heart
To see her love, her joy, again.
She had no wish now to retain
Anger toward him, she confessed.
Then rumour, that never rests
But flies about unceasingly,
Reached the queen, most suddenly,
That, for her sake, Lancelot would
Have slain himself, if he but could.
She feels delight, and thinks it so,
And yet for naught would have it so,
Too great a sorrow it had brought.
But Lancelot had reached the court,
Arriving swiftly, and in haste,
And now the king ran to embrace
Him, and kissed him on sight.
He felt as if he would take flight,
Light-hearted, full of joy was he,
But joy did fade, when he did see
Those who'd made him prisoner.
The king said evilly they'd fare,
For all would now be put to death.
And they responded with one breath
That they had thought he wished it so.
'Tis I you have insulted though,'
Said the king, 'clear is his name;
To him you have brought no shame,
Only to me his protector,
Shame is on me, and no other.

You'll find it no laughing matter,
When your heads are on a platter!'
Lancelot, at this angry speech,
Makes every effort now to preach
Peace and reconciliation;
And his firm determination
Meeting with success, the king
Him to Guinevere doth bring.
Now upon seeing the queen,
He sees she no longer means
To lower her eyes to the floor,
But meets his gaze as before,
Honouring him all she might;
Thus beside her sits the knight.
There they could talk at leisure
Of whatever gave them pleasure,
Nor did their speech fail them,
For Love did there regale them.
And when Lancelot saw that he
Could indeed say naught but pleased
The queen, in confidence, he said:
'Lady, I wonder why, instead
Of this face, you turned to me
Your other face, when you did see
Me, the day before yesterday,
Nor had a single word to say.
Never a word to me you said,
Such that I was almost dead.
Nor had I the courage to ask
Why I was so taken to task,
As I dare now ask it of you.
For I will make amends, anew,
If you will only choose to say
What fault of mine caused your dismay.'
And the queen spoke again:

'What? Did you not hesitate, then,
To mount upon the cart, for shame?
Were you not loath to do that same,
And thus for two whole steps delayed?
That, in truth, is why I repaid
You, by denying word or glance.'
'In future, in such circumstance,
May God save me from like folly,'
He said: 'may God deny me mercy,
If you were not, then, in the right.
For God's sake, lady,' said the knight,
'At once receive amends from me,
And if I might e'er pardoned be,
Then, for God's sake, tell me now!'
'Friend, said the queen, 'Thus I vow,
That of your guilt you shall be free;
I pardon you most willingly.
'Lady,' he said, 'my thanks to you,
Yet here I cannot say to you
All indeed that I wish to say,
I would speak with you if I may
At greater leisure; soon or late.'
To him the queen doth indicate
A window, with a glance of her eye,
'Come speak with me,' she doth reply,
'At the window, there, tonight,
When you deem all asleep, sir knight.
Come through the garden secretly;
Think not to enter bodily,
Such is not possible, I mean;
You'll be without, and I within.
Think not that any man may enter;
I may yet touch you however,
With my lips and with my hand.
And, if it please, you understand,

I'll stay till morn for love for you.
But more than this we cannot do,
For in the room, and close by me,
Lies Kay, the Seneschal, for he
Languishes there, of his wounds.
Closed is the door to the room,
Tightly bolted and guarded well.
When you come, take care, I tell
You, that of you none have sight.'
'If I can, lady,' said the knight
 I'll make sure none spy on me,
Who might evil think or speak.'
Thus having talked, heart to heart,
Filled with joy, they both depart.

LINES 4531-4650 THE TRYST BY NIGHT

FROM the room went Lancelot,
So joyfully that he forgot
All about his troubles quite,
Yet so impatient for the night,
It seemed that the day was longer
Than if he'd been forced to suffer
A hundred others, or a year.
He would have sought to appear
Before her, if only it were night!
Yet conquering, at last, the light,
A darkness, deep and shadowy,
Wrapped day in its mystery,
To lie beneath its cloak, all hid.
Once of the daylight he was rid,
He feigned to be good and tired,
And claimed he must now retire

For he was much in need of sleep.
But you, who do such vigil keep,
Know that he was merely waiting
For all the folk in his lodging
To think him slumbering in repose.
Yet he would not sleep, God knows,
Nor for his bed hath any care;
He cannot now, nor would he dare
Do so, nor, as he waits the hour,
Desires the courage or the power.
Not long after he rose quietly,
Nor was he disturbed unduly
That moon nor star shone bright,
Nor, in his lodgings, candlelight;
Neither lamp not lantern burned.
Outside, here and there he turned,
But none was there to see him,
All within thought him sleeping,
In his bed throughout the night.
Without an escort thus, our knight
Swiftly went toward the garden,
Meeting none, nor seeking pardon,
And to his good fortune found
A stretch of wall lay on the ground,
Where it had fallen recently.
Through this he passed silently,
And proceeded till he came
To the window, the very same;
There he stood, quiet as you please,
Seeking not to cough or sneeze,
Unmoving, taking every care,
Until the queen arrived there,
In the whitest white chemise,
No coat or cloak had she seized,
But thrown a short cape about her,

Of scarlet cloth and dormouse fur.
As soon as Lancelot saw the queen,
Who at the window-sill did lean,
Behind cruel iron bars stationed,
He gave her a gentle salutation.
And she him greeting did offer,
Both desirous of each other,
Both he of she, and she of he.
They speak no triviality,
Nothing tiresome do they say.
Each to the other strains alway,
As they clasp each other's hand;
So distressed, you understand,
At being near, and yet so far,
That they curse those iron bars.
But Lancelot claims, boastfully,
That if the queen will but agree
He'll be inside at once with her,
Nor iron bars keep him from her.
And to him the queen replies:
'Do you not see their strength and size,
Hard to bend, and hard to shatter?
You could never twist and batter
Pull, or draw them, this I know,
As ever to dislodge them so.'
'Lady,' said he, 'now do not quail!
These bars will prove of no avail;
Naught but yourself will hinder me
From embracing you completely.
If you will but grant your leave
The way is open here for me,
Though if you should not agree
Then is it blocked so utterly
There is no path I might follow.'
'Your wish,' she says, 'is mine, and so

My consent need not detain you,
But, a moment now, restrain you,
Till I may seek my bed again,
That no mischief may you pain;
For twould be no jest, I fear,
If the Seneschal, who lies here,
Hearing a noise, should awake.
It must be right that I betake
Myself to bed, since I do fear
Much ill, should he find me here.'
'Go then, my lady,' he replies
But have no fear at all that I
Will make the slightest noise at all;
So soft I'll draw these bars withal,
And, as I work, such care I'll take,
That not one person shall awake.'

LINES 4651-4754 LANCELOT IN THE QUEEN'S BED

THEN the queen, silently, withdrew,
While Lancelot prepared to do
His utmost to unbar the window,
Grasping, wrenching, tugging so
That the bars bent at their base,
And he could draw them from their place.
But so very sharp the bars were
That the tip of his little finger
Was sliced almost to the bone,
And then the first joint alone
Of the next was well-nigh severed.
But to the blood, they delivered,
And the wounds he paid no heed;
His mind on other things indeed.

The window's not so very low,
Yet through it Lancelot doth go,
Most swiftly, and right easily.
There he finds Kay, sleeping soundly,
And seeks the bed where lies the queen,
Whom he adores, and doth esteem
More than the relicts of some saint.
There the queen doth him acquaint
With her embrace, and he doth rest,
Clasped so tightly against her breast,
He's drawn into the bed, beside her,
Where she her fairest gifts delivers
To him, the sweetest that she can,
And Love and the heart grant a man.
Love would have her treat him so,
Yet, if she loves, he doth also,
A thousand times as much as her;
And Love is lacking in every other
Heart, compared to the love in his,
For Love has so entered into this
Man's heart, Love doth it so fill,
That all other hearts Love treats ill.
Thus has Lancelot all his wish,
Now the queen doth freely relish
His affection, and company,
Now in his arms he holds her tightly,
And she in her arms him doth greet.
So is their play both fine and sweet;
And such the kisses they employ,
Without a lie, they feel such joy,
A joy so marvellous, that never
Was its equal delivered ever,
Or has e'er been known or heard.
But silence upon it be conferred,
For in story it must not be told.

Of the joys which this pair enfold
The most delightful and choice
Are those our tale denies a voice.
More of such joy and delight
Did Lancelot enjoy that night.
But day comes, sorrow its bride,
For he must leave his lover's side.
On rising, it costs him such pain
To leave her, and depart again,
It seems to him pure martyrdom.
His heart disdains to be gone,
And with the queen doth remain.
He has no power now to reclaim
His heart, for so the queen doth please
It would not have its pleasure cease;
The heart remains, the body goes.
Straight to the window they chose
He returns, but enough remains
Of his body, for his blood stains
The sheets, fallen from his fingers.
Lancelot now no longer lingers,
Departing full of sighs and tears.
No time has been set, he fears,
For them to meet; it cannot be.
He leaves by the window, sadly,
Where he so gladly did enter,
Wounded now in each finger,
So badly had he cut them there.
Yet still the bars he doth repair,
And sets them in their former place,
So that whichever way one face,
Toward the one or the other side,
It seems no one has ever tried
To dislodge or remove the bars.
When from there he doth depart,

'But day comes, sorrow its bride,
For he must leave his lover's side.'
The Blue Poetry Book (p140, 1891)
Andrew Lang (1844-1912), H. J. Ford (1860-1941)
and Lancelot Speed (1860–1931)
Internet Archive Book Images

He bows, as a man doth incline
Before the altar, or a shrine;
Then goes, in great anguish still,
And meets none he knows until
To his lodgings he doth come.
There, without waking anyone,
He threw himself naked on his bed,
Wondering that his fingers bled,
From the wounds that he'd received.
Yet by these he was not grieved,
For he was certain in his mind
That any wounds that he might find
Were made when he'd drawn the bars.
And he was less concerned by far
Than he might have been if he
Had entered not; would rather be
Lacking both his arms, indeed.
Yet if through any other deed
He had been hurt so grievously,
Sad would he have been, and angry.

LINES 4755-5006 KAY THE SENESCHAL, STANDS WRONGFULLY ACCUSED

NEXT morn the queen lay deep in slumber;
There, within her curtained chamber.
Sweet sleep had overtaken her,
Of the bloodied sheets unaware,
For though stained with Lancelot's blood,
She knew not but they were good,
White, clean, and presentable.
Now, as soon as he was able,
Up and dressed, all elegant,

To the chamber, Meleagant,
Made his way, and found the queen
Full wide awake, and, readily seen,
Spots of fresh blood on the white.
He showed them to his fellow knights,
Then he, suspecting ill alway,
Looked to the Seneschal, Kay,
And saw his sheets blood-stained,
For that night, I should explain,
All his wounds had oped again.
'Lady,' he cried, 'Now do I gain
Such evidence as I desired!
Truly, in folly is that man mired
Who a woman would confine,
He wastes his effort and his time;
For he who guards her loses her
Sooner than he who ignores her.
A fine watch upon you has kept
My father, gainst me, while you slept!
He has guarded you well from me,
Yet Kay, looking on you freely,
In spite of him, this past night,
Of you had satisfaction quite,
As may be proven, readily.'
'How?' she cried. 'Here I may see,
Blood on your sheets, true witness,
Such that they lead me to express
My conclusion; by them I know,
From this my proof, that it is so;
The spots on your sheets, and on his,
From his wounds, are witnesses.'
Then the queen seeing, as he said,
Bloodstains there on either bed,
Wondered at them, and with shame
She blushed, her cheeks all aflame,

And said: So help me God, the stain
Upon these sheets, I do maintain,
Was not made here by Sir Kay;
But my nose bled ere light of day;
From my nose the blood did fall.'
She thinking it the truth, withal.
'Upon my life,' said Meleagant,
'There is naught in that, I'll grant;
There is no need for lying words,
For now you're caught, I do aver,
And the truth I soon shall prove.'
Then he said: 'Sirs, do not move!'
To the guardsmen standing there,
'Till I return, do you have care
These sheets remain upon the bed.
I shall have justice, as I have said,
When the king has seen this thing.'
He searched till he had found the king,
And, kneeling at his feet, he cried:
'Come, see what cannot be denied,
Sire, how your defence has failed.
Come and see the queen you jailed,
See the evidence, true and sound,
For I'll reveal what I have found.
But ere you go, I pray that you,
Both right and justice there will do,
And that you'll do so without fail.
You well know the sore travail
I've undertaken for the queen,
Yet you my enemy have seemed,
Who under guard keep her from me.
This very morn I went to see
Her in her chamber, and did view
Her bed, and proved it to be true
That Kay lies with her every night.

Sire, by God, am I not right
Thus to be troubled and complain?
Be not angered, for I'm disdained
By one who scorns me, and hates me,
While Kay's to lie with her nightly.'
'Quiet!' said the king, ''Tis but deceit.'
'Then come, Sire, and view the sheet,
See the trail Lord Kay doth leave.
Since my words you'll not believe,
And even seem to think I lie,
Sheet and quilt will meet your eye
Stained with blood from his wound,
All will be still as there I found.'
'Then, let us go, now,' said the king,
'For I wish to verify this thing:
My eyes will judge of the truth.'
So the king goes to see the proof,
Into the chamber, where he finds
The queen who rises, at his sign.
He sees the blood upon her sheets,
And Kay's alike, and her he greets
With: 'This is ill, if tis as he said,'
And she replies: 'God be my aid,
Never, even in dream, has so
Evil a lie been spoken. No,
I'd deem that Kay, the Seneschal,
Is so courteous and so loyal,
He'd ne'er commit such a deed.
As I'd not expose myself, indeed,
In the market-place, no more would I
Offer my body to any that try.
Kay's not the man for such outrage,
Nor have I wish to encourage
Such a thing, nor would do so ever.'
'Sire,' said Meleagant, 'to his father,

'I'd be much obliged to you if Kay
 For this outrage were made to pay,
And the queen exposed to shame.
Justice I now request and claim,
Justice is yours thus to declare,
Kay has betrayed King Arthur there.
His lord who so believed in him
Had entrusted the queen to him,
The thing he loves most, say I.'
'Sire, suffer me now to reply,
And exonerate myself,' said Kay.
When my soul flees, on that day,
May God deny to it His mercy,
If ever I lay with my lady.
I would rather be dead and gone,
Than ever such vile and ugly wrong
Commit toward my lord and master.
And may God never grant better
Health to me than I now possess;
Kill me rather, inflict no less,
If such a thought e'er came to me.
Rather my wounds bled profusely,
As I lay, last night, in my bed,
Thus my sheets they dyed all red.
For that your son doth me indite,
Yet, to do so, he hath no right.'
And Meleagant to him replied:
'So help me God, devils, say I,
And evil spirits have you betrayed.
Last night, heated and disarrayed,
Your exertions and your excess
Have opened your wounds afresh.
Your denial does you no good,
On both beds the trail of blood
Is evident, your guilt we see.

Right it is that whoe'er may be
Caught, openly, in such a way,
For his crime should swiftly pay.
So famed a knight did ne'er commit
Such baseness, shame on you for it.'
'Sire, sire,' to the king, cried Kay,
'Against what your son doth say
I'll defend myself and the lady.
Pain and distress he causes me,
Yet he is wrong to treat me so.'
'To fight my son would harm you though,'
Said the king, 'you are wounded still.'
'Sire,' he answered, 'though I am ill,
I'll fight with him, if you so allow,
And prove to all men here, I vow,
That I am not guilty of the shame
With which he would mar my name.'
Meanwhile the queen to Lancelot,
All secretly, her word had got,
And told the king she would send
A knight who would Sir Kay defend
From the charge, gainst Meleagant,
If, in his pride, he'd not recant.
And Meleagant at once replied:
'There is no knight I e'er espied
I'd shrink from meeting in a fight,
Till one of us be conquered quite,
Not if he were a giant, indeed.'
Then Lancelot appeared, and he
Brought with him such a rout of knights
They filled the great hall outright.
As soon as he had entered, the queen
Told young and old upon the scene
The nature of the thing, and she
Cried: 'Lancelot, this infamy

Meleagant will impute to me,
And claim I lie, this falsity,
Before all here, to be a fact,
If you do not make him now retract.
Last night indeed, he claims, Sir Kay
Lay with me, for he doth display
My sheets and his all stained with blood.
And says that therefore Kay should
Be charged unless he can defend
Himself, or if he wishes, a friend,
On his behalf, stand forth and fight.'
'You need not ask it,' said the knight,
'Where'er I am, such is your right.
May it ne'er be pleasing in the sight
Of God, that you or Kay should e'er
Be discredited, in this affair.
I'm ready to prove, in battle's court,
That he ne'er harboured such a thought.
For Kay I'll fight, with all my power
And defend him mightily this hour.'
Then Meleagant leapt to his feet,
And said: 'So help me God, I'll meet
With him, it pleases in all respects,
And let none think that I object.'
Lancelot said: 'Sir King, before,
I've met with lawsuits, and the law,
And with pleas and judgements too.
We should not fight without us two
Swearing an oath, in such a case.'
Meleagant replied, from his place,
And answered him, immediately:
'I will swear, most willingly;
Bring the saint's relics ere we fight,
For I know well that I am right!'
And Lancelot answered him again:

Chrétien De Troyes

'So help me God, I here maintain,
He knoweth not the Seneschal,
Who'd him, in this, a liar call.'
Then their steeds they demanded,
That arms be sought they commanded;
All was brought prompt to the assay;
The valets arm them; armed are they.
The holy relics are brought to bear,
Meleagant, his oath to swear,
Steps forward, Lancelot equally,
And both men fall to their knees;
Then Meleagant lays his hands
On the relics, as truth demands:
'So help me God, and this saint,
The Seneschal, tis my complaint,
Lay with the queen, all last night,
And of her, then, took his delight.'
'And I take you for a perjurer;
He touched her not, nor lay with her,'
Cries Lancelot, 'and so I swear,
And may a vengeful God not spare
Him who lies, and may he bring
The truth to light anent this thing.
Moreover I will take another
Oath, and swear that, whomever
It displeases and doth annoy,
If this day should bring me joy,
And Meleagant I should conquer,
So help me God and none other
Except the saint whose bones I see,
I'll show to this knight no mercy.'
But when this latter oath he heard,
The king took no joy in its words.

LINES 5007-5198 GAWAIN AT THE SUNKEN BRIDGE

ONCE their oaths have been duly sworn,
Their horses, fine and nobly born,
Are brought forward, and proudly shown,
While each man now mounts his own.
Then against each other they ride,
As swiftly as their steeds will fly.
When their steeds are in mid-course
They seek each other to unhorse,
So that not a fragment is left
Of the stout lances that they heft.
Each brings the other to the ground,
Yet their wounds are not profound,
For each knight rises to his feet,
And he the other knight doth meet,
Each with his bright naked sword.
Then sparks from their helms upward
Fly high towards the sky above.
So hot and fiercely do they move,
The naked blades in their hands,
That as now, to and fro, each man
Strikes, encountering the other,
Both are so enmeshed together,
They dare not pause to take a breath.
The king fearful of his son's death,
Now called aloud to the queen,
Who in the tower could be seen
At a window, watching on high:
'By God, the Creator,' thus he cried,
'Let these two men be kept apart!'
'Whate'er is dear to your heart,

Replied the queen, 'in honesty,
Meets no objection from me.'
Now Lancelot it seems had heard
The queen's answer, every word,
To this request made by the king,
And so he sought now to bring
An end to it, and cease outright;
But Meleagant maintained the fight,
Struck at him, and would not rest.
So the king toward them pressed
And seized his son, who yet swore
He wished no peace, but as before:
'I seek to fight, no peace for me.'
And the king said: 'Come, quietly,
Listen to me if you'd prove wise.
No hurt or shame now I apprise
Will come to you if you obey,
And do now as you ought this day!
Recall you not that you agreed
To fight again, and are indeed
Destined for King Arthur's court?
And see you not that to have fought
And conquered will bring you, there,
Much greater honour than elsewhere?'
Thus the king, to see if he could
So influence him that he would
Be appeased, and the knights part.
While Lancelot, with all his heart,
Wishing to go and find Gawain,
Did, to the king, his need explain,
Asking his, and the queen's, leave.
And, this granted, taking his leave,
To the Sunken Bridge made his way,
While to accompany him that day,
There followed a host of armed men.

Though he'd have preferred, again,
If most of them had stayed behind.
Down many a road they did wind,
Till the Sunken Bridge was nigh,
A league off, hidden from the eye;
Yet, before they reached the place,
Upon a horse, fit for the chase,
A dwarf it was who came in sight,
Holding a whip with which he might
Spur on his great hunter, at need,
And to the chase incite his steed.
Doing as he had been commanded,
Of the knights, he now demanded:
'Which of you men is Lancelot?
I'm of your party; hide him not;
For assuredly, be it understood,
I ask you thus for your own good.'
Lancelot replied, in his own right,
Saying: 'I am that very knight
Whom you enquire for, and see.'
'Ah! Honest knight, trust in me,'
Said the dwarf, 'quit this company,
And, all alone, come you with me,
For I'll lead you to a goodly place;
Let none follow you now apace,
But let them wait here patiently,
Until we return, and presently.'
Lancelot, suspecting no ill,
Bids all his men wait there still,
And after this false dwarf doth fare;
While all his men, remaining there,
Must await him, long time indeed,
For those folk who him have seized,
Wish not to render him again.
His men are in such grief and pain,

At Lancelot's failure to return,
They know not which way to turn.
They all say the dwarf's a traitor,
And, sadly, that to enquire after
Him would prove to be in vain.
Yet they begin to search again,
Though how to find him they know not,
Nor where to seek for Lancelot;
So they take counsel together.
Then among them, one or other,
Of the most rational and wise,
Persuaded them, as I surmise,
To go to the Sunken Bridge nigh,
And if they could find thereby
My Lord Gawain, in wood or plain,
With him, renew the search again.
With this they were all in accord;
So much so there was no discord.
Towards the Sunken Bridge they went,
Thus rewarded in their intent,
For my Lord Gawain they saw,
Fallen from the Bridge, before,
Into the water which was deep.
Now he sinks, and now doth leap,
Now they see him, now he's lost.
But with branches, at the cost
Of some effort, with hook and pole,
They raise him, from the watery hole.
He'd his chain-mail; on his head
A helmet worth more, it is said,
Than ten others; his greaves too,
Stained with sweat, of rusty hue;
For he had suffered much travail,
Of trials and perils great the tale,
Which he had passed and tamed.

His lance and shield yet remained,
With his horse, on the other shore.
Whether he lived they were unsure,
As they dragged him from the depths;
Water he'd swallowed in excess,
And until his lungs were clear
Not a word from him did they hear.
But once the weight was off his heart,
His throat, and mouth, and every part,
And once they heard and understood
All those sounds of speech he could
Deliver, and what they might mean;
Twas news he sought, of the queen,
And whether those who stood around
Had of her gained sight or sound.
And those who answered him replied
That yet at King Bademagu's side
She remained, and that with honour
He treated her, and waited on her.
'Has none yet sought for her again,
In this land?' said my Lord Gawain.
'Yes' they answered him. 'And who?'
'Lancelot of the Lake, passed through,
O'er the Bridge of the Sword, ere he
Rescued her, and thus set her free,
And with her all the rest of us;
Yet we're betrayed by a vicious,
Humpbacked, pot-bellied, dwarf,
Who deceived us, without remorse,
Seducing Lancelot away,
Nor do we know now what he may
Have done with him.' 'When?' said Gawain.
'Today, so wrought that devil's bane,
Near this place, when with Lancelot
In company for you we sought.'

'And how has he been occupied
Since in this land he did reside?'
And so their tale began to flow,
All was told him, blow by blow,
Not forgetting a single word,
And thus of the queen he heard,
Who awaited him, 'and tis true,'
They said, 'that till she sees you
She'll not depart from this land,
Till news of you comes to hand.'
My Lord Gawain then replied,
'When from this bridge we ride,
Shall we not seek for Lancelot?'
Not one of them would rather not,
Preferring to go and see the queen,
And let the king seek him. Between
Them they deem that the king's son
Meleagant, holds him in prison,
For, treacherous, he hates him so.
Yet if the king comes to know
Of it, he'll force him to free
Lancelot, of a surety.

LINES 5199-5256 KING BADEMAGU INITIATES A SEARCH FOR LANCELOT

WITH this counsel they all agreed,
And rode away, full swiftly indeed,
Till their company reached the court
Where the king and queen they sought,
And found them with the Seneschal,
Sir Kay, and also that disloyal
Son, so filled with treachery

Who'd caused such great anxiety,
Among those who now arrived.
They feel betrayed, scarce alive,
Sadness on them weighs heavily.
Tis not news filled with courtesy,
That thus brings sorrow on the queen;
Nevertheless she still is seen
To bear herself as best she may.
She resolves to endure the day,
For the sake of my Lord Gawain,
Yet she cannot so hide her pain
As to conceal its hurt completely.
Joy and sadness must mingled be:
For Lancelot, her heart is pained,
And yet, before my Lord Gawain,
She must show an excess of joy.
All must feel sadness, unalloyed,
Who hear the news that Lancelot
Is lost, for such cannot be forgot.
The king indeed would have been
Delighted that he now had seen
Gawain, and made his acquaintance,
Were he not so sad at the absence
Of Lancelot, lost and betrayed,
Which saw him utterly dismayed.
And Queen Guinevere begs the king
To send out men to search for him,
Here and there and up and down,
Without delay, till he is found.
And my Lord Gawain, and Kay,
Beg too, and all, in their array,
Add their prayers and requests.
'Leave this to me and for the rest
Speak no more of it!' said the king.
'I have arranged that very thing;

Without another word or prayer,
He shall be sought for everywhere.'
All bowed to him in gratitude,
While he his own commands issued;
Messengers now scoured the land
The wisest men, of those to hand,
Who went about the whole country
Seeking what news there might be.
They made enquiry everywhere
But no certain news was there.
Finding none they return again
To where Kay and my Lord Gawain
Wait for them, among the knights,
Who all declare, armed for the fight,
Lances levelled, that they will go,
Nor send another to seek him so.

LINES 5257-5378 THE FORGED LETTER

ON a day, after they had all
Eaten, they armed, in the hall,
And had reached the moment where
Naught was to do but onward fare,
When a valet entered the place,
Passing among them till he faced
The queen, Guinevere, whose colour
Seemed scarcely healthy, however,
For she was grieving for Lancelot,
Not knowing if he lived or not,
So deeply, that her looks were pale.
Then the valet the queen did hail,
And the king who was by her side,
And then the rest who stood nearby,

And Kay and then my Lord Gawain.
He held a letter, that much was plain,
Which he now offered to the king,
Who asked a man of true learning
To read the letter to all those there,
For he, who did its contents share,
Knew how to voice whate'er he read.
Lancelot sent greetings, he said,
To the king as his good master,
And thanked him for the honour
He had done him, and the service,
As one who, on account of this,
Was forever at his command.
The king was now to understand
That he was at King Arthur's court,
And all safe and sound, in short,
And that he bid the queen come there,
If she would do so, in the care
Of my Lord Gawain and Sir Kay.
In proof of which he affixed that day,
His seal, which they should know, and did.
Much joy was now exhibited:
All the court echoed with delight,
And on the morrow, when twas light,
They said, they would indeed depart.
And so they all prepared to start,
And were ready at break of day.
They rise and mount and are away,
And with great joy and ceremony
The king doth them accompany,
For a good distance on the way.
To the border he doth convey
Their party, and when he has seen
Them safe, takes leave of the queen
And then, indeed, of all the rest.

The queen most courteously expressed
Her thanks for kindnesses received,
To the king, as he took his leave.
She threw her arms about his neck,
Offered and promised her respect,
Her service, and that of her lord:
Nor indeed could she offer more.
And then my Lord Gawain also
Promised his services, and so
Did Kay, as to a lord and friend,
And then the king did commend
Them to God, ere they rode away.
After these three, the king did pay
Respects to all, and turned for home.
Not for a day did the queen roam,
Straying from the road, or tarry,
Until to the court they might carry
News of her, and her company,
News that doth make Arthur happy,
On hearing of his queen's approach;
He for his nephew has no reproach
But joy at heart and great delight,
Thinking that by his skill the knight
Has brought about the queen's return;
And Kay's and all, he hopes to learn.
But the truth was other than he thought.
Emptied is both the town and court,
As all there go to encounter
The company and, all together,
Whether true knights or vassals plain,
Cry: 'Welcome to my Lord Gawain,
Who brings the queen, in company
With many a once-captive lady
Whom from prison he doth render!'
And Gawain replied, in answer:

'Gentlemen, now praise me not
Let your compliments be forgot,
For naught is attributable to me.
Such acclaim brings shame on me,
For I reached not the queen in time,
My own delay must seem a crime.
But Lancelot came there indeed,
And has such honour by his deed,
As not another knight has won.'
'Fair sir, where is he then, the one
You speak of, for we see him not?'
'Where?' said Gawain: 'at the court
Of my lord the king, is he not here?'
'No, by my faith, he is not, I fear,
Nor in this country for many a day;
For since my lady was led away
Of Lancelot we've had no word.'
Gawain, hearing, at once inferred
That the letter was false, and they
Had been deceived and betrayed;
All misled by a traiterous letter.
Then their grief indeed was bitter,
And grieving they came to court.
Where at once King Arthur sought
News concerning the whole affair.
Many a man could tell him there,
All that Sir Lancelot had done,
And how he had freed from prison
The queen herself and all the rest,
And with what treachery his guest
The dwarf had then stolen away.
And all this did the king dismay,
And much sorrow and grief it brought.
But his heart felt joy at the thought
Of the queen's return, such that he

Found joy eclipsing misery.
Now that he had what he loved best,
He cared little for all the rest.

LINES 5379-5514 LANCELOT HEARS NEWS OF THE TOURNAMENT

WHILE the queen was, as I believe,
Out of the country, she did leave
Many a maid disconsolate,
Many a lady, and their debate
Had them declare that they would
Be wed as soon as e'er they could.
And this being now their intent,
They agreed they would foment
A contest, and arrange a tourney;
The lady of Pomelegloi to see
To this, with the lady of Noauz.
They'd have naught to do with those
Who fared ill, but would receive
In marriage those who did achieve
Something worthy on that field.
Its date the criers now revealed
To all the countryside nearby
And all that furthest from the eye,
Giving the time well in advance
And every other circumstance,
So that more folk would thus attend.
And now the queen returned again
Before the date that they had set;
As soon as they heard, they met,
And knowing the queen was there
Most to the court did then repair,

And, finding the king was at court,
Once before him, they all sought
That a favour he might bestow,
And fulfil their every longing so.
And the king promised them this,
Before he even knew their wish;
Thus he'd grant all they required.
Then they told him they desired
That he should allow the queen
To, presently, attend the scene.
He, unaccustomed to say no,
Said yes, if they wished it so.
So, gratified and well-content,
Off to see the queen, they went,
And said to her, immediately:
'Do not deprive us now, lady,
Of all that the king has granted.'
And when the queen demanded:
'What then? Hide it not from me!'
They answered: 'To our tourney
If you should desire to come,
He will not keep you at home,
And nor will he quarrel with it.'
Then she said that she would visit
Since the king had given her leave.
Through all the realm, I do believe,
Those ladies sent word that they
Would bring the queen on the day
They had announced formerly,
On which the tournament would be.
The news travelled everywhere,
Far and wide, here and there,
Until, progressing on its way,
It came to where that kingdom lay
From which, before, none returned,

But now to which whoever learned
Of it had entry, and might leave,
And no challenge would receive.
Far throughout that country went
The latest news of their intent,
Until it reached a seneschal,
Of Maleagant, the disloyal,
The traitor, whom may hellfire burn!
This man had Lancelot interned,
Entrusted with his captivity
By Meleagant, whose enmity
Towards Lancelot was great.
The latter learned now of the date
And the hour of the tournament,
Nor were his eyes then innocent
Of tears, nor indeed his heart light.
Seeing the sad and pensive knight,
The lady of the house in person
Offered him counsel and wisdom:
'Sir, for God's and your soul's sake,
Tell me truly,' she said, 'what makes
You sad, and whence this change in you?
Both food and drink you now refuse,
I see you neither laugh nor smile.
You may tell me, without guile,
Of those thoughts that trouble you.'
'Ah, lady! If I'm sad, for true
It is, by God, be not surprised.
Grieving I go, with downcast eyes,
For that brave field I shall not see
Where the best in the world must be,
At the tourney, where all assemble,
It seems to me, whom I resemble.
Nevertheless, if you so pleased,
If God would set your mind at ease,

Such that you let me travel there,
Then be assured, to you I swear,
That I would behave such that I
Should return to you, by and by.'
'Surely I would, most willingly,'
She said, 'were it not that I see
In that my death and destruction,
So greatly do I fear the actions
Of Meleagant, our vile master,
Thus I dare not; such disaster
It would bring upon my lord.
No wonder if we fear his sword,
For evil he is, as well you know.'
'Lady, if you still fear though
That after the tournament there
I'll not return, then will I swear
On oath to you, for your own sake,
An oath that I will never break,
That there is naught that shall detain
Me from returning here again
As soon as the tourney is done.'
'I'faith,' said she, 'I have but one
Condition.' 'What is that, lady?'
'Sir, that you will swear to me
To return, but promise no less
Than that your love I'll possess.'
He answered her, without pause:
'Lady, all that I have is yours,
And I do swear to return here.'
'Then shall I have naught, I fear,'
Said the lady, full of laughter,
'For I know that to another
You have pledged and granted
The very love that I demanded.
Nevertheless, I'll not disdain

To take whatever may remain.
Thus I will keep all that I can,
And your assurances command,
That you will prove true to me,
And return to your captivity.'

LINES 5515-5594 LANCELOT TRAVELS TO THE TOURNEY AND FINDS LODGINGS

SUBMITTING to this lady's law,
By Holy Church Lancelot swore
He would return thus, without fail.
Then the lady lent him the mail
And vermilion arms of her lord,
And his war-horse did him afford,
Wondrous fine, and brave, and strong.
He thanked her, mounted, and was gone,
Splendid in his fine new armour,
Armed with weapons, riding ever
Until to Noauz he came.
There, concealing his true name,
He took lodgings near the town.
Never has such a great man found
So poor and low a dwelling-place;
But, there, he would avoid his face
Being recognised, and so his name.
Many a knight well-known to fame
Were gathered there in the town,
Yet many others lodged around;
For so many flocked to that affair
Since the queen herself was there,
A fifth part had to dwell outside.
For every one who would so ride

To tourney, there were seven who
Were there because the queen was too.
For a good five leagues around
The barons lay about the town,
In lodges, tents and pavilions.
And twas a wonder, all the sum
Of maidens and fine ladies there.
Outside his lodgings' door, with care,
Lancelot had placed his shield.
And then his armour he did yield
For comfort, and so down he lay
On the bed, which in every way
He disdained, for it was narrow,
The mattress thin, to his sorrow,
With but a coarse hemp coverlet.
Thus disarmed, while he as yet
Still lay there in his poor estate,
A fellow came, as he did wait;
A shirt-sleeved herald-at-arms,
Who to the tavern and its charms
Had left his coat and his shoes
As a pledge, barefoot, abused
By the wind, came at the trot;
He saw this shield of Lancelot's
Before the door, but knew it not,
For though he gazed he'd never
Seen it, and knew not its master,
Nor who might here be its bearer.
The door lay open to any farer,
And, entering, on the bed he saw
Lancelot there, and what is more
Crossed himself for he knew him.
And Lancelot gazed hard at him,
Then ordered him to say naught
Of it, where'er he was, at court

Or elsewhere; for if he should say
A word, better for him that day
If he were blinded, or his neck
Were broken. 'Sire, in great respect
I ever held you, and shall do still,
And so, as I live, I never will,'
Said the herald, 'do aught that may
Bring you displeasure in any way.'
Then from the house he did go
Crying aloud, both high and low:
'Here comes one who'll take your measure!
Here comes one who'll take your measure!'
He went crying it everywhere,
And all the folk they came to stare
And ask the meaning of his cry.
But not so rash as to reply,
He went on calling out the same,
From his mouth the same cry came:
'Here comes one who'll take your measure!'
The herald granted us that treasure,
He taught us all to say the phrase,
Who used it first in olden days.

LINES 5595-5640 THE CROWD GATHERS

NOW there gathered for the tourney,
The queen herself and all her ladies,
And all the knights and other folk,
And men-at-arms, there to invoke
The rules, in all parts, left and right.
Near the place where they would fight,
Here were stands, built from wood,
Where, near the queen, there sat or stood

All the maidens, and the ladies;
There were never seen so many
Stands, so large 'and finely-made,
Where all the women now displayed
Themselves, drawn there by the queen,
Wishing to see, while being seen,
Which knights fared better or worse.
The knights arrived in tens at first,
Then in twenties, thirties, and more,
Eight there, and ninety they saw,
A hundred plus, and yonder yet
Twice the number; so many met
Before the stands, and all around,
The commencement now did sound.
Armed, unarmed, they all assembled;
Their lances a forest resembled,
For those knights come to the sport
Had so many weapons brought
There was naught on that scene
But lances, standards, to be seen.
The jousters then the joust began,
Each finding many another man
Arrived there with the same intent;
While others sought to represent
The various skills of chivalry.
So full of knights were the fields,
The meadows and the untilled land,
To seek the number there on hand
Was idle, none could count the lot.
And yet no sign of Lancelot
Was seen at this first encounter,
But when he came, a little later,
The herald, seeing him nearby,
Could not then forebear to cry:
'Here comes one who'll take your measure!

Here comes one who'll take your measure!'
Then 'Who is he?' the folk did cry,
But not a word would he reply.

LINES 5641-6104 THE TOURNAMENT

WHEN Lancelot now made his entry
He was worth of knights the twenty
Best, so well there did he fight,
Such that all must turn their sight
On him, wherever he might be.
For Pomelegloi fought valiantly
A brave and most skilful knight,
While faster than a stag in flight
Was his steed, that tall did stand;
He was a king's son, of Ireland,
And well and handsomely did ride,
But many times more they sighed
For him whose name they knew not,
Hastening to ask whence or what
He was: 'He fights well, who is he?'
Meanwhile the queen, most covertly,
Spoke to her maid, both wise and clever,
'A message now you must deliver,
She said, and do it now and swiftly,
And in brief words, and privately.
Go down quickly from the stand
And find the knight there on hand
Who carries a vermilion shield,
And secretly this message yield
That 'au noauz', he do his 'worst'.
Swiftly, but cautiously at first,
The maid did as the queen wished;

For as soon as she'd accomplished
The finding of him, she stood close
And in a voice, so soft and low
That his neighbours could not hear,
'The queen, sir,' whispered in his ear,
'Sends you these words, by me,
To do your worst.' 'Most willingly,'
On hearing her words, he replied,
Like one all hers, and then did ride
Against another knight as swiftly
As his steed would go, while he
Deliberately missed his thrust.
And from that moment until dusk
He fought as badly as he could
As the queen desired he should.
And yet the other knight made no
Mistake, and struck him such a blow,
That Lancelot indeed took flight;
Nor that day toward any knight
Did he now turn his horse's head;
On pain of death he chose instead
To do naught that day unless he
Shame in its outcome did foresee,
And deep disgrace and dishonour,
And, moreover, he feigned terror,
As the knights passed to and fro.
And the very men who had so
Prized Sir Lancelot, formerly,
Now mocked this knight, derisively,
And the herald who was wont to cry:
'He'll beat them all now, by and by!'
Was baffled and discomfited,
Hearing all that, in jest, they said,
With utter scorn: 'Be silent, friend,
His measure-taking is at an end,

So much he's measured of this host,
His measure's done for, and your boast.'
Many said: 'What will he do now?
For he seemed brave, you must allow,
Yet now appears so cowardly,
He turns from every knight he sees.
He seemed so fine, you may be sure,
Because he'd never fought before,
In his first onslaught was so strong
None could withstand him among
All the great host of knights, in short
Fought as a wild man might have fought.
Now of arms he has learnt so much
Doubtless he'll not dare to touch
Arms again, his whole life through.
His heart could not endure it, true,
For none's as cowardly as his.'
And the queen, watching all this,
Was pleased, nay delighted, in short,
For she knew, though she said naught,
That he, in truth, was Lancelot.
Thus all the day, till day was not,
Lancelot played the coward's part,
Until near vespers all did depart.
On leaving there was much debate
As to who had fought best to date.
Thus the king of Ireland's son
Thought, despite contradiction,
He'd won the glory and renown.
Yet he did not deserve the crown,
Many there had proved his equal.
Even that knight had pleased all
The ladies and the maids, at first,
And of those fairest not the worst,
He with the vermilion armour,

Such that they'd watched him more
Than any other, seeing how well
He then fought, and how skilful
And brave he had seemed to be.
Though then he'd proved cowardly,
And dared not face a single knight,
Till even the humblest in the fight,
Could defeat him if they wished.
And they, at their departure, insist
They will return on the morrow,
And will choose, for joy or sorrow,
Those who win honours that day,
As their husbands, come what may.
All folk then to their lodgings go,
And, reaching their lodgings so,
Demand of each other, outright:
'What has become of that knight,
The worst and the most despised?
Where did he go to? Where hide?
Where to seek, how to ascertain?
Doubtless we'll ne'er see him again,
Whom Cowardice has chased away,
That of which he's so full, I say,
There's none as cowardly as he.
Nor is he wrong, for the cowardly
Are a hundred times more at ease
Than fighting men, if you please.
Cowardice is pleasant and easy,
Thus in peace he kissed her sweetly,
And had from her whate'er she had.
But Courage proves never so bad
As to lodge herself with such a one,
Or close, as Cowardice has done,
For she has lodged with him entire,
And found the host she doth desire,

Who'll so honour her, and serve,
He'll forsake his honour for her.'
Thus all night they slander him,
Competing to speak ill of him,
Though men oft slander another
Who are worse than their brother
They pour shame on and despise.
All spoke of him and in such wise.
And with the dawn on the next day
The crowd, returned to the display,
All gathered at the jousting-place.
And to the stand the queen retraced
Her steps, and the ladies and maids,
And with them there were arrayed
Unarmed knights, whom they treated
As captives, having been defeated,
Who gave the arms, shield by shield,
Of those they prized most in the field,
Remarking: 'See him who doth hold
That shield there with band of gold
On a red field; full brave and quick
Is Governauz of Roberdic.
And there, not far from him, another
Who, on the shield at his shoulder,
Bears an eagle and a dragon?
He's son to the King of Aragon,
And to this country he has come
That fame and honour might be won.
See, of his neighbour I can tell,
He who thrusts and jousts so well,
Half his shield is painted green,
On that a leopard may be seen,
The other half is clear azure;
Tis Ignaures, whom all adore,
He's both amorous and pleasant.

He who with pheasant to pheasant,
Beak to beak, his shield doth deck?
That's Coguillanz of Mautirec.
And see those two next each other
On dappled greys, like as brothers,
A lion black on each gold shield?
The one his name I cannot yield,
But his dear friend is Semiramis,
And like shields they bear in this.
Then do you see he that, in state,
Bears on his shield an open gate,
With a stag issuing from it there.
I'faith, that knight is King Ider.'
Thus, high in the stands, they gloze:
'That shield was made in Limoges,
Brought here today by Pilades;
He loves tourneys such as these,
Eager for battle, win or lose.
That other was made at Toulouse,
The breast-strap, and bridle also,
Brought here by Kay of Estrau.
That came from Lyons on the Rhone,
Under heaven no better's known,
Given for merit and so proffered
To that knight, Taulas of the Desert,
Who bears it well, and skilfully.
That other was worked artfully
In England, and in London made,
A pair of swallows there displayed,
That seem as if about to fly,
But never move, yet feel, say I,
Many a Poitevin lance and more;
And he is Thoas, called the Poor.
So they describe and explicate
The coats of arms of those they rate.

But of him they catch no sight
Whom they hold in such despite,
Suspecting he has slipped away
Finding him absent from the fray;
While the queen on seeing him not
Considers if he should be sought
Amongst the crowd till he is found.
She knows of none better to sound
Than she whom she sent his way,
With her message, but yesterday.
So calling the maiden to her side
'Go, demoiselle,' she says, 'go ride,
Mount your palfrey, and search for
That knight to whom I sent before,
But yesterday, go search and find.
Linger here for naught else, mind;
To him repeat your last refrain,
Tell him to do his worst again.
And, when you've done so, then, say I,
Attend full closely to his reply.'
The maiden suffered no delay,
For she indeed recalled the way
He had gone the evening before,
And she had known that more
Than once she'd be asked to go.
And thus through the ranks she rode,
Till she came across the knight
Whom at once she bade to fight,
But do his worst and ever waver,
If he wished the love and favour
Of the queen, which she now brought.
And he: 'Whatever twas she sought
Would win my thanks, is my reply!'
The maiden leaves him, by and by,
Then valets, sergeants, squires, begin

To raise a shout, amidst the din,
Crying: 'Now, behold this wonder,
The knight in the vermilion armour
Is here again. What can he wish?'
For ne'er so vile a knight as he,
So worthless and so cowardly,
Exists in all the world, this hour.
Cowardice has him in her power,
Such that he cannot oppose her.'
Meanwhile the maid herself doth stir
To hasten, and inform the queen,
Who keeps her close by, I ween,
Asking her what says the knight.
Then her heart fills with delight,
Knowing now, whate'er befall,
That it is him to whom she's all,
And she his own, without fail.
She tells the maiden she must sail
Swiftly to him, and must say
The queen doth command him, pray,
To do the best now that he can.
And she says she'll find the man
Again, and now, without delay.
From the stand, she makes her way
To where the lad waits patiently,
Keeping tight hold of her palfrey,
And she mounts, and off she rides
Till she finds him where he bides,
The knight, to whom at once says she:
'Sir, the word now from my lady,
Is you must do 'the best' you can!'
And he replied: 'I am her man;
Tell her tis no hardship ever
To do her will, for whatever
Pleases her, that's my delight.'

'*Show all his skill and his prowess.*
His horse he doth now address'
St. Nicholas [serial] (p558, 1873)
Mary Mapes Dodge (1830-1905)
Internet Archive Book Images

Nor was the maiden slow in flight
Returning to the queen, for she
Thought indeed his words would greatly
Please, and so delight, the queen.
As soon then as she could, I ween,
She made her way towards the stand
And the queen, seeing at her hand,
Rose swiftly, and went to greet her,
Yet did not descend, to meet her,
Waiting at the head of the stair.
So the maid approached her there,
Happy her message to recount,
And thus the stair she did mount,
And once she had reached its head:
'Lady I never saw,' she said,
'A knight quite so debonair,
And one so eager, in this affair,
To do whatever it is you ask,
For truth be told, whate'er the task,
He accepts, with the same face,
Good or ill, and ever with grace.
'T'faith, she said, 'good let it be.'
Then back to the window went she,
To gaze again at all the knights.
And Lancelot, swift as he might,
Seized his shield by the leathers,
Desiring to display his feathers,
Show all his skill and his prowess.
His horse he doth now address
And runs him between the lines.
Soon they'll be troubled in mind
The misguided and deluded men
Who all day long, and then again
At night, heaped him with ridicule.
Much have they played the fool,

'*Then knights fly out, spurring on*'
St. Nicholas [serial] (p558, 1873)
Mary Mapes Dodge (1830-1905)
Internet Archive Book Images

Disporting themselves in fun.
Now the King of Ireland's son
Gripping his own shield tightly,
Spurs apace, galloping lightly,
To meet him in close encounter.
So fiercely do they come together,
That the son of the Irish king
His lance, thereby splintering,
Seeks no more of the tournament,
For Lancelot blunted his intent;
It was no mossy board he struck,
But good hard wood to his ill luck,
And Lancelot thus did him harm,
Pinning his shield to his left arm,
Pinning his arm then to his side,
Downing his horse to end his ride.
Then knights fly out, spurring on
From either side, to the king's son,
One party to save him from distress,
The other to savour their success.
These men think to aid their lord,
While many are lost overboard,
Their saddles emptied in the fray.
And yet absent from that melee,
Was Gawain, his weapons at rest,
Though he was there, with the best,
For such pleasure did he take
In all the moves the knight did make,
With arms and armour painted red,
Others' deeds seemed pale instead,
And failed indeed to compare,
With all the red knight did there.
The herald now was full of cheer,
Shouting aloud so all could hear:
'Now he's here to take your measure!

'*And the maidens who with wonder Watched him*'
St. Nicholas [serial] (p460, 1873)
Mary Mapes Dodge (1830-1905)
Internet Archive Book Images

Today you'll marvel, at your leisure.
Today his prowess shall appear.'
Then the knight his steed did veer,
And made a very skilful thrust,
And laid a knight there in the dust,
Hurled from his steed so far, be sure
He sailed a hundred feet or more.
Lancelot commenced his advance,
With the sword and with the lance,
So well, that none watching there,
Failed to delight in that affair.
And many an armed knight indeed
Found pleasure in Lancelot's deeds.
It was fine sport to watch how he
Floored horse and rider with ease,
Tumbling to the ground together.
Hardly a knight did he encounter
Who in his saddle still remained,
While the mounts he thereby gained
He gave to whomever he desired.
Those who taunts and jibes had sired,
At his expense, said: 'Shamed are we,
And mortified; fools, utterly,
To deride and vilify this knight,
For he is worth a thousand quite
Of such as those upon this field,
For he conquers and makes yield
Every knight that meets with him,
Such that none will fight with him.'
And the maidens who with wonder
Watched him said to one another
That he might take them now to wife,
For none there trusted, on her life,
In her beauty, or her dower,
Or her status, or her power;

For not for their wealth or beauty
Would this knight seek to marry
Any there, such was his prowess.
Yet most of them, nevertheless,
Are so enamoured of the man
They declare that, except they can
Wed with him, they'll not be wed
To any other lord instead.
And the queen who hears it all,
All the words that they let fall,
Smiles to herself with delight
For she knows that this knight
Were he to have before him set
All Arabia's gold, would yet
Refuse the best, the most fair,
The noblest of the maidens there;
Not one of them would he take,
Not one of them, for her dear sake.
One wish is common, each alone
Would yet have him for her own;
And each is filled with jealousy
As if her husband now is he,
All because of his great prowess
In the field, such that all confess
No knight in arms, nary a one,
Could e'er do as he has done.
So fine his deeds, as he departs
All say, without a lie, his arts
Are such that he of the red shield
Has no equal, upon that field.
All spoke of it and it was true,
Yet in the lists as he withdrew
He left his shield, there where he
The centre of the crowd did see,
And his trappings and his lance,

Then took himself to a distance;
So swift he went, so secretly,
That none gathered there did see
Him leave, which way he went,
Nor noticed that he was absent,
Swift and sure to that very same
Place, he rode, from which he came,
In order to fulfil his oath.
At the tourney, the knights both
Asked for him, and likewise sought
Where he might be, and yet naught
Found of one who'd not be known.
Great sorrow and distress they own,
Who if they could have found the knight
Would have greeted him with delight.
Yet if the knights now feel dismay
That he has left them thus this day,
The maidens, when they also knew,
Felt greater sorrow and, anew,
They swore that they, by Saint John,
Would ne'er, that year, wed anyone,
And if denied the man they wished
Then all the rest must be dismissed.
Thus the tournament has ended,
Without their finding their intended.
And Lancelot to the road doth turn,
Soon to his prison to return.
But its seneschal reached the spot,
Two or three days ere Lancelot,
And asked where he might be.
And the lady who had freely
Loaned him the accoutrements,
Had his vermilion armour lent,
His horse and harness and all,
Confessed all to the seneschal;

And how she had sent him so
To the tournament at Noauz;
All the truth she did rehearse.
'You could have done no worse,
My lady,' said the seneschal.
'In truth, I doubt not, I shall
Suffer for all this, and my lord
Meleagant shall to me afford
Less aid than sailors in distress
Win from the cruel and merciless.
Dead, or in exile, I shall be.
He will show no pity to me.'
'Now, fair sir, be not dismayed,
He will not halt, or be delayed,'
Said the lady, 'so have no fear,
For you need not, he will appear;
By all the saints, he swore he would
Return as swiftly as he could.'

LINES 6105-6166 LANCELOT IS IMPRISONED IN THE TOWER

NOW the seneschal mounts his horse
And comes to his lord, in due course,
And tells him all the sorry tale.
But reassures him without fail,
That Lancelot, upon his life,
Has sworn an oath to his wife
That to prison he will return.
'I know,' said Meleagant, in turn,
'That his word he will not break,
Nonetheless, your wife's mistake
Fills me with displeasure, withal.
I'd not have him, for aught at all,

Present now at that tournament,
But go now, make it your intent
That once he is with you again,
His liberty he'll not regain;
Hold him tightly then in prison,
His body deprived of freedom.
And make sure to send me word.'
'Thus shall I do, as I have heard.'
The seneschal, on leaving, learned,
That Lancelot had now returned,
And was a prisoner in his court.
Therefore he sent a brief report
Swiftly flying on its way
To Meleagant, which did say
To his liege lord that Lancelot
Had now returned. On learning what
That message contained, his master
Gathered masons and carpenters,
Who would or must do his bidding.
The country's finest summoning,
He ordered them to fashion there
A tower, and give it all their care,
And build it well and skilfully.
The stone was quarried by the sea,
For on this side, and close to Gorre
There is an island, set offshore
In a long wide stretch of water,
Of which Meleagant was master.
Thus the stone was carried over,
And all materials for the tower.
In less than two months, I'd say,
The tower was fit in every way,
Well-founded, strong, and tall.
When his men had seen to all,
Lancelot was brought, by night,

And prisoned there, out of sight.
Then they walled up the door,
And all the masons duly swore
That they, forever and a day,
Naught of that tower would say.
For Meleagant wished it sealed,
Such that its bare walls revealed
But one small window that remained.
Within, Lancelot is detained,
And but poor and meagre fare
Is delivered to him there,
Through the tiny window's grate,
At certain hours, as they dictate,
Thus he is treated cruelly,
By that master of treachery.

Lines 6167-6220 Meleagant issues the summons

Now, all being done as required,
Meleagant, at once, desired
To take himself to Arthur's court.
There, behold, he is now brought,
And as he stands before the king,
Bold, arrogant in everything,
He begins his speech, and says:
'King, before you, in this place,
I do hereby summon Lancelot
To a contest, but see him not,
Who did agree to meet me here.
Nevertheless, as all now hear,
In the presence of those I see,
I offer to fight, as is my duty.
If he is present, let him appear,

And to his agreement adhere
In a year's time at your court.
I know not if any have sought
To tell in what manner or guise
This agreement was realised,
But I see knights I might mention
Who were there at its inception,
And are here today, who could
Tell you the truth, if they would.
Should he deny it, before me,
I'd employ none other, but he
Upon his body would see it proved.'
The queen, who was seated, moved
To draw to her the king beside her,
And to him she now did murmur:
'Sire, know you not who this is?
Meleagant, who did me seize
Besides Sir Kay the Seneschal,
Bringing him much shame and ill.'
And the king straight replied to her:
'Lady, I well know who stands there;
I see that it is the one, no less,
Who held my people in duress.'
The queen said not another word,
But the king, having thus conferred,
Toward Meleagant turned his head:
'God save me, friend,' the king said,
Of Lancelot now we have had no
News, indeed it brings us sorrow.
'King and sire,' said Meleagant,
'Lancelot told me he would stand
Here, to meet me, without fail.
And nowhere else might I avail
Myself of the oath that he swore,
But at your court, and all these lords

Shall bear true witness to what I say:
I summon him, a year from today,
To the battle here, thus decreed
When the covenant was agreed.'

LINES 6221-6458 KING BADEMAGU'S DAUGHTER
PLANS TO FREE LANCELOT

AT his words, Gawain now rose
Grieved by what he had disclosed,
Troubled by all that he had heard:
'Sire, of Lancelot not a word
Has come to us in all this land,
But we shall set a search on hand
And, if God please, he will be here
Before the last day of the year,
Unless he's dead or in prison.
If he cannot attend in person
Grant me the contest; I will fight,
For Lancelot I'll act the knight
If he returns not ere that day.'
'Ah! By God,' this boon, I pray,
Which he desires, do you grant,
To him, for I' said Meleagant,
'Know not of any other knight,
In all the world, I'd rather fight
Except for Lancelot alone,
Of a surety, let it be known:
If I fight not one of these two
I'll meet no other substitute,
For one of the pair it must be.'
And the king did so agree,
If Lancelot failed to appear.

Meleagant now left his peers,
Parting from King Arthur's court,
For now indeed he sought,
His father King Bademagu.
Once before him, to pursue
The appearance of bravery,
He feigned an air of jollity,
A happy face did now employ.
That day the king full of joy
Held court at Bade, his city.
Twas the day of his nativity,
So he was fine and generous,
While full many and various
Were those who there did gather.
The palace was in high fever,
All full of maidens and knights;
And one of the maidens bright
Was sister to Meleagant;
Of her I'll not speak in advance
Of my thoughts and intention,
Here I'll make no further mention
Of her, for I'd not confuse
My matter but instead I choose
Not to muddle things mid-course,
Nor interrupt my true discourse,
But keep to the straight and narrow.
And so I now will have you know
That Meleagant in his father's hall
In all men's hearing, great or small,
Said to his father, clear and loud:
'So help me God, do tell me now,
And tell me truly, if you please,
Is he not the seat of bravery,
Should not that man be full of joy,
Who, at the threat that he'll employ

His arms, brings fear to Arthur's court?'
His father, then, without a thought,
To his question at once replied:
'My son, no good man can deny
That he should e'er honour and serve
One who doth such respect deserve,
And seek out that man's company.'
Then begged him, using flattery,
To say, and naught from him conceal,
Why to him he doth thus appeal,
His wishes, and whence come hither.
'Sire, I know not if you remember,'
Said his son, Meleagant,
'The conditions and the covenant
Which were recorded and agreed,
When your terms we did concede,
Lancelot and I together.
We committed, one and the other,
It seems to me, and before all,
That, ere a year, should befall
We'd fight at King Arthur's court.
At the due time, there, I sought
Him; I myself ready, waiting
For whate'er my fate might bring.
Thus all that I ought I have done,
For Lancelot I searched, but none
Had seen him, that I might fight,
And yet of him had nary a sight;
He had hidden himself or fled.
When I came away, twas said
By Sir Gawain, in pledge to me,
If Lancelot was dead, and he
Could not within the time set
Thus appear, then even yet
No respite would be sought,

But he himself, before the court,
Would fight in place of Lancelot.
Arthur not one knight has got,
As all men know, as fine as he;
But ere the springtime we shall see,
When he and I attempt that same,
Whether his deeds match his fame;
And I would wish to prove it now!'
'Son,' said his father, 'I do avow,
You seek to play the fool, for sure.
Any who knew it not before,
May learn of it from your own lips.
A good heart doth itself eclipse,
Bows low, but that the boastful fool
Ne'er ends his folly, tis the rule.
Son, as for you, now, I do say,
That your own self it is alway
So harsh and dry that I do see
No sweetness there, nor amity.
Your heart all devoid of pity,
You are wholly gripped by folly.
Tis why I do chastise you so,
Tis what, indeed, will lay you low.
If you are brave, men will concede
That very same, whene'er you need.
The virtuous man seeks not to praise
His courage that his actions may
Seem greater; they themselves extol.
Self-praise will not achieve your goal
Of advancing in men's esteem,
One jot; no, it lessens you, I deem.
Son, I reprove you; to what end?
Tis vain to hope a fool will mend.
He wastes his strength utterly
Who'd rid a fool of his folly.

All the wisdom men expound,
Is worthless if it be not found
To bring reform; wasted, lost.'
Meleagant, being thus crossed,
Now sore enraged, waxed furious.
I may say that never, among us,
Could you see man born of woman
As full of anger as was this man,
And now the last bond he broke
Between them, as these words he spoke
Ungraciously, to his father
Seeking not to yield or flatter:
'Are you asleep, or do you dream,
You who claim that mad I seem
Who speak but of my situation?
I thought to a father I had come,
As to my lord and my master,
But that appears untrue, rather
You insult me, outrageously,
Beyond all right, it seems to me,
Nor can you give any reason
For treating me with derision.'
'I can indeed.' 'What reason then?'
'That I see naught in you, again,
But anger, and foolishness.
I know you've courage in excess,
And what ill it will bring to you.
Now cursed be any man who
Thinks Lancelot, the virtuous,
Who is so prized by all of us
Except for you, has fled from fear,
For I am certain it will appear
That he's buried, or held hard
In some prison, the door barred
So tight that he cannot leave.

Surely I would sorely grieve
If it should be the case that he
Is dead, or in sad captivity.
A mighty loss it would be
If a creature full of chivalry
So fine, so brave, so serene,
Vanished thus from the scene,
God please, it may not be true.'
Then words failed Bademagu.
But one of his daughters heard
What he had said, every word,
She listened to him thoughtfully,
And you must know that it was she
Whom I spoke of earlier, and
Is saddened now to understand
The likely fate of Lancelot.
It must surely be that he cannot
Be free, for news of him none know.
'May God not look upon me though,
She said, 'if I rest till I have found
Fresh trace of him, sight or sound;
Some news both certain and assured.'
Now, without waiting to hear more,
She, without noise, without murmur,
Leading it to a quiet corner,
Mounted a mule, fine, well-paced;
Though I must say she left that place
Not knowing the way she should go,
After departing the courtyard so.
She seeks no advice, travelling blind,
Taking the first road she doth find,
Riding swiftly, doth so adventure,
Not knowing where, at a venture,
Without knight or squire for guide.
Most eagerly, and with haste allied,

She seeks the object of her quest.
She presses on, and may not rest,
But her search will not end soon!
She may not rest, night or noon,
Nor linger in one place for long,
If she wishes to right this wrong,
As she herself has thought to do,
Can she but find, and then rescue
Lancelot, if she has the power.
But I think she'll first devour
Many a mile, in many a land,
Far and wide, on either hand,
Before fresh news of him she hears.
What point for me to fill your ears
With stories of inns and journeys,
The paths she rode were so many,
Both up and down, by hill and dale,
A month or more, upon the trail?
She'd learned nothing by it though
More than she before did know,
And that was nothing, certainly.
But one day, upon her journey,
Crossing a field, with a sigh,
She saw afar a tower set high
Upon the shore, beside the sea,
And there was not within a league
House or cottage or dwelling there.
And she was yet all unaware
That Meleagant had built it so
That Lancelot therein might go.
As soon as she had sight of it
She fixed all her gaze upon it,
Nor cast her two eyes elsewhere,
For her heart assured her, there
Lay the object that she sought.

Now she had reached the port,
To which Fortune had led her,
Once she had made her suffer.

LINES 6459-6656 LANCELOT IS FREED FROM PRISON

NOW the maid draws near the tower,
Till touching it's within her power.
She walks around it listening,
Gives her attention to the thing,
Seeking, I would think, to hear
Any sound that meets the ear.
She looks down and to the sky:
The tower is solid, strong, and high;
Amazed to find but one narrow
Opening, a little window,
And no sign there of a door.
Around the tower, what's more,
Is neither scaffolding nor stair.
She therefore thinks it made with care
To prison Lancelot inside,
But, ere she eats, she will try
To find if it is true or not.
She thinks to call out 'Lancelot',
And so summon him by name,
Yet ere she can pronounce the same,
She hears a voice that deters her,
A voice lamenting from the tower,
Marvellously sad, its breath
Calling upon naught but death.
Death it seeks, 'too great' its cry,
'Too great these ills' and longs to die:
Life and the body it despises,

Condemning them, the voice rises,
But weakly, both hoarse and low,
'Ah! Fortune, how your wheel hath, so
Disastrously, turned for me!
You have mocked me shamefully,
For I was up and now am down;
I who was well, now ill am found.
Once you smiled, now you weep,
Why did you faith with one keep,
Poor wretch, who deserts you so!
A moment and she brings you low.
Truly 'the depths from the height':
To scorn you Fortune is not right.
I wrought ill, but what care you?
Tis naught to you what doth ensue.
Oh! Sacred Cross, oh, Holy Ghost,
How I am lost, half-dead almost!
How, in all, now, from all, I fall!
Ah Gawain, matched by none at all
In goodness, of such worth are you,
I wonder why your help, tis due,
Comes not; why you deny me aid?
For sure, your help is long delayed,
And thus you show scant courtesy!
Your aid he ought now to receive
He to whom such love you showed!
For in truth I would have followed,
Sought to find where you might be
On this or that side of the sea,
Where'er you were, on either shore,
A good ten years at least, and more,
If you were in prison, and I knew,
Ere I would thus abandon you.
But why do I with myself debate?
You care too little about my fate,

To wish to trouble yourself so.
The saying's true, all men do know,
Tis hard these days to find a friend.
On whom, that is, we may depend,
We swiftly prove in time of need.
More than a year has passed, indeed,
Alas, since I was here enclosed.
And I feel such pain, God knows,
That you, Gawain, have not sought
To find me; mayhap you know naught,
Yet I seek to lay the blame on you.
I see it clearly; it must be true,
My ill thoughts I now abjure,
For, thinking on it, I am sure
Heaven and earth, without fail,
You'd move to free me from this gaol,
From this misfortune, and constraint,
Without your needing my complaint,
If but the truth your ears had found.
Indeed, to do so you'd be bound
From love and friendship no less,
If no other reason you'd profess.
But this is naught, such cannot be.
May he who has so shamefully
Prisoned me, be damned forever,
By God and by Saint Sylvester!
The vilest man alive is he,
This Meleagant, who of envy
Has done me all the ill he can!'
To silence then returns the man
Who wears away his life in grief.
But when she, who waits beneath
The window, hears all he doth say
She seeks to act, without delay,
Knowing now what she must do,

She calls to him, and wisely too:
'Lancelot!' Loudly as she can,
'Friend above,' calls to the man,
Speak now to your friend below!'
He fails to hear her calling so.
She calls again and louder yet,
Until he hears at last, and yet
Wonders, in his weakness, who
It could be, as she calls anew.
He heard the voice, and its call,
But knew not who it was at all:
He thought a spirit it might be.
He looked around so as to see
Its source, but saw, at that hour,
Naught but himself and the tower.
'God,' said he, 'what's this I hear?
The sound is speech, yet none are here!
I'faith, tis more than marvellous;
Since I sleep not, well then I must
Be wide awake; were it in dream
A mere illusion it would seem;
But I'm awake, at which I grieve.'
Then painfully he rose to leave
The spot and so, little by little,
Went towards the window-sill.
Once he was there he spied
Up and down, and side to side,
All outside, the best he might,
Till of the maiden he had sight.
He knew her not, but him she knew;
Thus she said: 'Lancelot, for you,
From afar, I've come in search;
God be thanked, for my search
Is over, and I've found you now.
I'm she to whom you did allow,

As to the Bridge of the Sword
You went, a plea, and did accord
Me a boon, when I asked of you:
It was the head I sought, that you
Cut from the knight that I did fear,
Whom at no time did I hold dear.
Because of that boon your guerdon
Is all this trouble to which I've gone,
And your reward is: I'll set you free.'
'Fair maid,' he said, 'I'll thankful be,
If you can pluck me from prison,
Then shall I have a pretty guerdon
For that small service rendered you,
If I can from this tower issue.
If you can bring me liberty,
I promise and engage to be
Yours forever, by the Gospel,
And Saint Paul the Apostle!
And, if I'd see God face to face,
No day there'll be that I'll not grace
With whate'er you may demand.
Naught there is that I command
But you may ask for it any day,
It will be yours without delay.'
'Friend, you shall be, do not fear,
Released from this prison here.
You shall be freed this very day;
Not for a thousand livres, I say,
Would I see you here one day more;
Then to a better place, be sure,
I shall bring you, where you may rest.
There shall you have whate'er is best
What pleases you, it shall be yours.
Therefore trouble yourself no more:
But first I must by searching trace

Chrétien De Troyes

Where there might be, in this place,
Some lever, with which, once found,
You might this narrow window sound,
Such that through it you might pass.'
'God grant you find the thing, my lass!'
Said he, commending thus her plan;
'And I have plenty of rope to hand,
Which my gaolers have given me
To drag aloft my food, hard barley
Bread, and buckets of foul water,
That harm my body, fair daughter.'
Then that child of Bademagu
Sought out a pick, a sharp one too,
Strong and sound, roped it, and he
Raised it, then grasping it tightly
Hammered and struck, despite the pain,
Till a wide opening he did gain,
Through which he issued easily.
He was delighted to be free,
As you'll imagine, now that he,
Having achieved his liberty,
Was removed from that ward
Where so long he'd been immured.
Now he's at large, in the clear air,
Nor would wish to be back there,
Not if all the gold in the world
Was in one pile together hurled,
You understand, and to him given,
With all the silver under heaven.

LINES 6657-6728 LANCELOT IS RESTORED BY THE MAIDENS' CARE

BEHOLD, released is Lancelot,
And yet to stumble is his lot,
From weakness and feebleness.
Without causing him distress,
On her mule she sets him though,
And quickly on their way they go,
Except the byways she doth try,
That none may see them passing by,
And takes the hidden paths, for fear
If travelling openly they appear,
And then are seen and recognised,
Dire harm would thus be realised,
Such is not what she doth wish.
From the open road they vanish,
To reach at last a mansion where
She often stays; she doth repair
To it for its charm and beauty.
And this retreat was hers entirely
With its people; and twas the case,
That well-furnished was the place,
And healthy, private, and secure.
She brought Lancelot to her door,
As soon as he had entered there,
And shed his clothes, pale and bare,
The maiden placed the knight gently
On a couch both fine and lofty,
Then she bathed and massaged him
So scrupulously, limb by limb,
I could not tell of half her care.

She treats him as gently there
As if he might be her father:
Tends to him, him doth alter,
Renewing him, so wondrously,
Now fair as an angel is he,
And more fit and lively, say I,
Than any that you could espy;
No longer haggard now and pale,
But handsome and strong and hale.
And now for him the maiden sought
The finest robes, and these she brought
To clothe him now, as he arose;
And gladly he donned the clothes,
Swift as a bird doth soar in flight.
Kissing the maiden then the knight
Said to her most graciously:
'I have but God and yourself only,
To render thanks to, my dear friend,
For my return to health again.
Since my escape from prison is due
To you, my heart, and body too,
And all my service and estate,
Whene'er you please, you may take.
Such deeds you've done, I am your own,
Yet long it is since I have shown
My face at King Arthur's court,
And much there is that I, in short,
Must do there; so, my sweet friend,
For Love, I pray you will extend
Me leave to go, that I may, then,
Go freely, and with your consent;
For he hath done me honour there.'
'Lancelot, friend most dear and fair,'
Said the maid, 'such is my desire,
For your good and honour, sire,

I wish above all, there and here.'
A wondrous steed she hath near,
Of all steeds known the very best,
This she gives him, and with zest,
Of stirrups taking small account,
Without a word now, up he mounts,
Then to God, He of falsehood free,
They commend each other, he and she.

LINES 6729-7004 LANCELOT RETURNS TO KING ARTHUR'S COURT

NOW Lancelot rode on his way
So joyfully, I swear, that day,
That I cannot describe the joy
He felt, delight without alloy,
That he was thus at liberty,
And freed from his captivity.
Yet he said often, and forcefully,
Woe to the traitor, who wrongfully
Had him in prison, one who now
He had fooled, as all must allow.
'For despite him I am at liberty.'
Then he did swear, soul and body,
By Him who made the world entire,
That not for the riches men desire,
The gold from Babylon to Ghent,
Would he free Meleagant, or relent,
If he held him, no, not for an hour,
When once he had him in his power,
For he had harmed him shamefully.
And that same thing may come to be,
For it so happened, as we now see,

217

That Meleagant himself whom he
Proposed to imprison when caught,
Had but that day arrived at court,
Unsummoned by anyone, and he'd
First sought where Gawain might be,
Found him, and asked for Lancelot,
And whether he'd been found or not,
The traitor making his request
As if upon some innocent quest,
Though he knew the facts he sought.
Yet, truth be told, he knew them not
Indeed, but only thought he knew.
Gawain informed him, as was true,
That he'd not come there, nor been seen.
'Since he's not to be found, I wean,'
Said Meleagant, 'then you must come
And keep the promise, and be done;
For I can no longer wait.'
Gawain said, 'I'll not hesitate,
If God please, in whom I trust,
To pay the debt, as well I must,
And I will keep my word to you,
And I'll not cease until I do,
For if it comes to keeping score,
And I do throw as many and more,
Then, by God and the Holy Faith,
I'll end all, and pocket the stakes.'
Then Gawain, without more ado,
The usual order doth issue;
Demands a carpet be unrolled,
And set before him, as of old.
Without demurring in any way,
At his command, the squires lay
The carpet where they are told.
There he sits, that place doth hold,

And orders them to fit his armour,
Those squires who do him honour,
Standing before him, at that spot,
Nephews or cousins, I know not,
But all accomplished, that is true.
And they knew all they had to do:
They armed him skilfully and well,
Such that none on earth could tell
Of any fault they could discover,
Nor could detect the slightest error
In anything that they had done.
When he was fully armed, then one
Of the squires brought a Spanish steed,
That could run more swiftly, indeed,
O'er hill and dale, by field and wood,
Than e'er the good Bucephalus could.
Such was the horse my Lord Gawain
Now mounted, he of noblest strain,
The finest knight the age displayed
O'er whom the sign of the Cross was made.
Yet as he prepared to grasp his shield,
There, before him, unexpectedly,
Lancelot, dismounting, appeared.
He gazed in wonder as he neared,
Since he'd arrived so suddenly,
As much surprised, believe me,
As if he'd wondrously descended
Upon him from the clouds, and ended
By standing there before him now.
Yet naught could stop him, I vow,
No greater business of his own,
On seeing tis none but he alone,
From leaping, himself, to the ground,
Embracing him, for he is found,
And welcoming him with a kiss.

Now has he joy, great ease in this,
Greeting thus his dear companion.
And I shall give my true opinion,
And, think you, what I say is not
Some tale: unless his Lancelot
Were with him, he would yet decline
To be crowned king, however fine.
Now the King heard, as did the rest,
That Lancelot whom, at his behest,
They'd long watched for, despite all
Had come safe and sound to the hall.
So they all rejoice together,
And those at court swiftly gather,
To welcome him they'd long looked for.
Great or small, they do him honour,
None there is lacks joy that day.
Their joy dispels and drives away
The sorrow that they felt before.
Grief doth flee, they joy the more,
Sadness replaced by true delight.
And did the queen enjoy the sight
Of Lancelot, and smile withal?
Yes, truly, she beyond them all.
How? Dear God, what felt she then,
If not the greatest joy again
She ever felt, at his return?
And did she not towards him turn?
In truth she did, and drew so near
That her body well-nigh, I fear,
Followed her heart, they were so close.
Where was the heart, do you suppose?
It kissed and embraced her Lancelot.
And why did the body touch him not?
Why was her joy incomplete?
Did anger or hatred there meet?

No, indeed, but twas lest, by chance,
The king might note the circumstance,
Or one of the other persons there,
Who were watching the whole affair,
Might on those two cast their eyes
And thus see all, if they were wise;
If she simply followed her heart.
Thus Reason kept the two apart,
For if it had not banished thence
Her wild thoughts, if common-sense
Had not concealed her heart's excess,
Revealed had been her foolishness.
So feelings Reason hid, and thought,
Restraining both, before the court,
Postponing the issue for a while,
Till it might, without undue guile,
Find some fine, more private place,
Where they might better embrace
Than where they were at that hour.
The king doth Lancelot endower
With honour, and after joyful word
Says: 'My friend, I have not heard
For a great while, word of anyone
That cheers my heart as this has done,
This news of you, but it troubles me
To know in what land, what country,
You have sojourned for so long.
All winter and all summer long
I've had men search, up and down,
But none, of you, had sight or sound.
'Indeed,' said Lancelot, 'fair sire,
Brief words may answer your desire,
As to how it has fared with me.
Meleagant, that fount of treachery,
Has held me far off, in prison,

Ever since that joyful season
When the prisoners were freed,
And in a tower, beside the sea,
Forced me to suffer great shame.
There by the power of his name,
I was, and would yet be, penned
If it were not for my dear friend,
A maiden, for whom I once did
Some small service, when she bid.
For that little gift I had done
She repaid me with large guerdon,
Bringing great good to Lancelot.
But that fellow whom I love not,
Who devised, and later wrought
Ill, and shame upon me brought,
Here and now, I would him repay,
All he deserves, without delay.
He comes to seek it; his shall it be.
He need not wait here endlessly,
For all is here at his own behest,
Both principal and interest.
But God be hoped he enjoy it not.'
Then said Gawain to Lancelot,
'The slightest favour it would be
If this debt were repaid by me,
Since I am ever in debt to you.
And I am already mounted too,
And all prepared as you may see.
Fair friend, do not deny it me,
This boon I do covet, moreover.'
But he replied he would rather
Lose an eye than forfeit there
His part in the present affair;
He swore that it could never be.
He owed the debt and it was he

Who would render it, faithfully.
Gawain who could clearly see
Naught he might say would avail,
Freed himself of his coat of mail,
And disarmed himself completely;
Lancelot arming himself swiftly,
For now he would brook no delay,
Impatient to settle, in his own way,
The debt he owed to Meleagant,
Who was amazed, in that instant,
Beyond measure, to see him there,
Before his eyes, and could but stare.
What he was owed he'd now receive,
Almost beside himself, indeed,
To fainting he came well-nigh.
'Surely,' said he, 'a fool was I
Not to go, before coming here,
And see if I still held him near,
In my prison, and in my tower;
He who has tricked me this hour.
Yet, my God, why should I so?
What reason had I to suppose
He might thus escape ere long?
Are not the walls good and strong,
Is not the tower sound and high?
There was no opening, to the eye,
Through which he might issue forth,
Unless he were aided of course.
His prison must have been revealed.
If the walls where he was concealed
Had fallen, and the tower grounded,
Would he not have been confounded
Trapped, and wounded or killed?
Yes, God help me, if so willed!
Thus he'd have died without fail;

But unless of force men did avail,
Before e'er those walls would falter,
The sea would dry and all its water
And not a drop be left, for sure,
Nor could the world itself endure.
That was not it, some other way
He was helped to the light of day.
Not otherwise could he have fled,
I have been tricked and so misled.
However it was, he's now abroad
Yet if I had kept him in closer ward,
None of this had happened though,
Nor at court would I see him so.
But tis too late now to repent,
The farmer says, with true intent,
And speaks the truth at his table,
In claiming it's too late the stable
Door to bolt, the horse being fled.
I know I've brought upon my head
Great shame and humiliation,
If not worse my expectation.
What must I suffer and endure?
Yet as long as I might live for
I will deal him measure enough,
Please God, in whom I place my trust.'
So he cheers himself and doth ask
Of himself no more than this task
That in the field they meet together.
He will not wait for long, however,
For Lancelot goes to seek him out,
Expecting the better of the bout.
But, before the contest may start,
The king requests that they depart
To the plain where a tower doth stand
The best place this side of Ireland

For a fight; and there do they go,
To meet on the plain down below.
The king goes there, and so too
All the rest, in a crowd, to view.
All depart, not one doth remain;
And to the tower windows, amain,
Go the queen, her maids and ladies,
Amongst whom are many beauties.

LINES 7005-7119 LANCELOT SLAYS MELEAGANT

IN the field stood a sycamore
As fair as any a tree, and more.
Its branches spread far and wide,
And it was ringed on every side
With short grass, fresh and fine,
Which was green all winter time.
Under this fine and noble tree,
Planted in Abel's century,
A little fountain from its spring
Sends its clear water issuing.
Its bed of translucent water,
Shines as brightly as silver,
And its channel, I would hold,
Is made of true refined gold;
And through the fields it doth sail
Between two woods, along a dale.
There sat the king, where all was green,
And nothing ill was to be seen.
The crowd were made to stand aside
Then Lancelot began his ride,
Against Meleagant, at speed,
As at one whom he hates indeed.

'*Then Lancelot began his ride, Against Meleagant, at speed*'
The Romance of King Arthur
and his Knights of the Round Table (p2, 1917)
Sir Thomas Malory (15th cent), Arthur Rackham (1867-1939)
and Alfred William Pollard (1859-1944)
Internet Archive Book Images

Yet first, ere he prepares to strike,
He shouts, as loudly as you like:
'I defy you, so now beware,
 For you, indeed, I shall not spare,
My word you have, it shall be so!'
An arrow's flight from the bow
He drew back, and then indeed
Most violently spurred on his steed.
Thus they let their mounts rush on,
Until the two knights meet head on,
And so furiously do they meet
That their lances loudly beat
Upon, and even pierce, the shields,
Yet, neither wounded neither yields,
The flesh untouched at first assault.
They pass, and then, without delay,
Return as fast as e'er they may,
Dealing mighty blows sidelong,
On those shields fine and strong;
For the knights give brave account,
And swift and hardy is each mount.
So fierce are the blows that peck
At those shields about their necks,
That the lances pierce right through,
And fail to break or splinter too
With such force through chain mesh
They glide, to reach the bare flesh.
Each strikes the other man so hard
That both men are borne earthward,
For no breast-strap, stirrup, or girth
Could save them from striking earth,
Knocked backward o'er the saddle-bow,
With but an empty saddle to show.
The horses are left to run astray,
Gone over the hills and far away.

One kicks hard, the other doth bite,
With mortal hatred, in their flight.
As for the knights, though grounded,
Swiftly to their feet they bounded,
And at once each drew his blade
That with letters was engraved,
Set his shield before his face,
And did the fight again embrace,
Seeking to make the other feel
The keen edge of his bright steel.
Lancelot feared no man that day,
For he knew more of swordplay
By far than his enemy, forsooth,
Having learnt well in his youth.
They each dealt such mighty blows
On each other's shields, God knows,
And on their helms barred with gold,
They shattered them, if truth be told.
But Lancelot pressed in strongly,
And launched such a blow that he
Struck Meleagant's mail-clad arm,
His right, all unshielded from harm,
And severed the arm at a stroke.
His enemy, at the pain, now spoke
Out at the loss; cried that its cost
Should be repaid, for dearly bought
It was, and its full price he sought;
For now with fury he did engage,
Beside himself with pain and rage,
And thought a wretch he must be
Could he not conquer this enemy.
He rushed at Lancelot, his intent
To seize him now, or such he meant,
But Lancelot forestalled his plan,
And with his sword dealt the man

'*Meleagant's done with and, dead*'
The Romance of King Arthur
and his Knights of the Round Table (p148, 1917)
Sir Thomas Malory (15th cent), Arthur Rackham (1867-1939)
and Alfred William Pollard (1859-1944)
Internet Archive Book Images

Such a blow he'd not recover
Till April and May were over;
Struck his nose-guard gainst his teeth,
Shattering three of them beneath.
And Meleagant felt such anger
That not a word could he utter.
A cry for mercy he doth disdain,
His foolish heart doth so constrain
His action still, and grips him tight.
Lancelot doth approach the knight,
Frees the helm, and takes his head.
Meleagant's done with and, dead,
He'll trouble Lancelot no more.
Nor shall any of those who saw
The battle, I now declare to you,
Feel pity at such a dreadful view.
The king and all the others there
Know great joy of the whole affair.
Happier than ever now they prove;
Lancelot's armour they remove,
And lead him away most joyfully.

LINES 7120-7134 GODEFROI'S ENVOI

MY Lords, did I prolong the story,
Beside the purpose it would seem,
Thus to its end I draw our theme:
Here the arrow doth find its mark.
Godefroi de Leigni, the clerk,
Has finished the Tale of the Cart;
But let none blame his feeble art
In completing Chrétien's intent,
For Chrétien gave it his consent.

He began it, and I, from where
Lancelot was imprisoned there,
Took up the story and my pen,
And so continue it to the end.
Such will I, but no further, sail,
Not least for fear I mar the tale.

The End of the Tale of Lancelot

ABOUT THE AUTHOR

Chrétien, likely a native of Troyes in north-eastern France, served at the court of his patroness, Marie of France, Countess of Champagne and daughter of Eleanor of Aquitaine, between 1160 and 1172. Hers was a literate court, and she herself knowledgeable in Latin as well as French texts, and Chrétien used the legendary court of King Arthur as an analogue for the French and Angevin courts of his own day. Marie's mother Eleanor became Queen of England, in 1154, as the spouse of Henry II, following annulment of her marriage to Louis VII of France, thus Chrétien was able to blend French and British traditions in his works. Between 1170 and 1190, Chrétien, writing in fluent octosyllabic couplets, developed and transformed the narrative verse tradition, and laid the foundations for the plot-driven prose narratives of later times.

ABOUT THE TRANSLATOR

Anthony Kline lives in England. He graduated in Mathematics from the University of Manchester, and was Chief Information Officer (Systems Director) of a large UK Company, before dedicating himself to his literary work and interests. He was born in 1947. His work consists of translations of poetry; critical works, biographical history with poetry as a central theme; and his own original poetry. He has translated into English from Latin, Ancient Greek, Classical Chinese and the European languages. He also maintains a deep interest in developments in Mathematics and the Sciences.

He continues to write predominantly for the Internet, making all works available in download format, with an added focus on the rapidly developing area of electronic books. His most extensive works are complete translations of Ovid's Metamorphoses and Dante's Divine Comedy.

Made in the USA
Las Vegas, NV
07 November 2021